The Weight of Finitude

SUNY series in
Hegelian Studies
William Desmond, editor

THE WEIGHT OF FINITUDE

On the Philosophical Question of God

by
Ludwig Heyde

translated by
Alexander Harmsen
and
William Desmond

foreword by
William Desmond

STATE UNIVERSITY OF NEW YORK PRESS

Originally published in the Netherlands by Boom
Under the title *Het gewicht van de eindigheid: Over de filosofische vraag naar God*
Copyright © 1995 L.C.M. Heyde, Nijmegen

The translation of this work was made possible by the financial support of National Fonds voor Wettenschappelijk Onderzoek (NWO, Netherlands)

Production by Ruth Fisher
Marketing by Anne M. Valentine

Published by
State University of New York Press, Albany

© 1999 State University of New York

For information, address the State University of New York Press,
State University Plaza, Albany, NY 12246

Library of Congress Cataloging-in-Publication Data

Heyde, Ludwig, 1941–
      [Gewicht van de eindigheid. English]
      The weight of finitude : on the pilosophical question of God / by Ludwig Heyde : translated by Alexander Harmsen and William Desmond.
            p.   cm. — (SUNY series in Hegelian Studies)
      Includes bibliographical references (p.   ) and index.
      ISBN 0-7914-4265-9 (hc. : alk. paper). — ISBN 0-7914-4266-7 (pbk. : alk. paper)
      1. God.   2. Religion—Philosophy.   I. Title.   II. Series.
BD573.H4513   1999
211—dc21   99-17957
                                                                                        CIP

10 9 8 7 6 5 4 3 2 1

*For An, Sophie,
and Marianne*

Contents

FOREWORD BY WILLIAM DESMOND   xi

PREFACE   xvii

INTRODUCTION   1

1   THE ABSENCE OF THE ESSENTIAL   9

1.1 *An Essenceless World*   10
     The Reversal of Positions   12
     The Dominion of Wealth   14
     Comedy and Cynicism   14
1.2 *The Protest of Faith*   15
     Faith as Flight   17
     The Essencelessness of Faith   17
1.3 *The "Retrieval"of the Essential. The Struggle of the*
     Enlightenment   20
     God's Disappearance   20
     The Unsatisfied Enlightenment   22
1.4 *A One-Dimensional World and a Distant God*   24

2   WAYS OF THINKING TOWARD GOD   29

2.1 *Faith and Thought*   29
     Faith   29
     The Experience of Thought   31
2.2 *Enigmatic Contingency*   33
     Why Something at all . . . ?   33

An Informational Intermezzo: Concerning Proofs of God 36

An Example: Thomas Aquinas 37

A Necessary Ground for All that is 39

The Decisive Presupposition 41

2.3 *The Actuality of Thought* 44

Intermezzo 44

Anselm. Thought and Being 45

Descartes. Subjectivity and Infinitude 48

God as Ground and Measure 50

2.4 *The Experience of Limits and Openness* 56

3 AN ABYSS FOR THOUGHT 61

3.1 *The Limits of Thought* 63

The Decisive Point: Thought and Being 63

Contingency 66

The Well-Ordered Cosmos 70

3.2 *The Scope of the Critique* 73

It Concerns the Entirety of Philosophy 73

The Ideal of Pure Reason 74

The Positive Turn 78

3.3 *Kant's Way: The Absoluteness of the Ought* 80

The Indisputable Moral "Fact" 82

The Postulate of God's Existence 84

3.4 *The Limits of the Limits* 87

Critique of the Critique 87

The Metaphysical Élan 91

4 AUSCHWITZ: THE END OF AN ILLUSION? 93

4.1 *The Mystery of Evil* 93

Beyond Any Concept? 93

The Sting of Moral Evil 97

4.2 *The Mystery of Freedom* 100

The Refusal of Adorno 101

Kant: Evil and Freedom 104

Contents

4.3 *The Rose and the Cross*   111
    God and Evil   111
    Evil is not Absolute   114

5   HUMAN FINITUDE AND THE PRESENCE OF GOD   117

5.1 *Finitude as Boundary*   120
    Heidegger: The Desacralisation of the World   120
    The Metaphysics of Subjectivity   125
    Thinking does not Merely "Happen" to Us   129
5.2 *The Mystery of God's Presence*   133
    The Death of God   133
    Nietzsche as Child of his Time   135
    Hegel: The Absolute is Present   136
    Finite Transcendence?   140
    Philosophy's Claim to Truth   142

NOTES   145
CITED LITERATURE   165
ABOUT THE AUTHOR   173
INDEX   175

Foreword
by William Desmond

Ludwig Heyde's book is a noteworthy exploration of a theme that has fallen into strange silence in our times. While there are numerous books written about religion, in many philosophical quarters one finds the implicit attitude that religion and philosophy have little to do with each other, and that the great preoccupation of the tradition of philosophy with the question of God is now behind us, and rightfully. With some exceptions, one can find this across the philosophical spectrum: from the Marxist ("mystification"), to the Nietzschean ("slave-morality"), the Heideggerian ("onto-theology"), the analytic philosopher ("woolly non-sense"), to the deconstructive postphilosopher("phallogocentrism").

Many factors, philosophical and extraphilosophical, could be adduced for this situation: secularization in the modern West, Kant's criticism of traditional metaphysics, overall narratives of history that consign religion to an earlier naive phase of humanity, such as we find in Comte and others, the rationalizing culture that sees the figurative representation of religion as inferior and as behind us, the Marxist critique, the psychoanalytical interpretation, Nietzsche's vehement passion that simply states it is not to our contemporary tastes, and in the very dismissiveness of the gesture embarrasses those who still in their heart of hearts are perplexed by the question of God.

With the weight of such factors pressing us down into the immanences of finitude, how could the soul take flight into a region formerly thought higher? We have been told we cannot fly, we have been ordered not to fly, we have only one wing, we have no wings, those misshapen feathery things are merely fantasms of our not-yet-enlightened imaginations, and anyway flying is really falling. Why then do some—perversely—insist on trying to fly?

Heyde wants to fly and yet he is not perverse. Quite to the contrary: in a multifacetted reflection, he gives the most careful attention to the major factors relevant to the question of God, both in the tradition and in more recent developments. He is struck into thought by wonder at the fact that what marks our time is indeed the absence of the essential. And what's more, too often it does not seem to bother anyone, even the philosophers! We seem to have become chirpily at home in the emptiness. Wonder at that most perplexing of perplexities seems to have gone on vacation.

Heyde's knowledge of the tradition of philosophy is outstanding. He is a highly respected writer on Hegel (in the Dutch-speaking world and beyond). Not surprisingly, Hegel is of great assistance to him in thinking through the matter. Heyde is not primarily concerned to give a comprehensive exegesis of Hegel, but to put to fruitful use some key Hegelian analyses, particularly in relation to faith and enlightenment. Our modern relation to the question of God takes shape here; nor is the postmodern free from this shape.

The claim is that we still inhabit such a cultural and spiritual configuration in which rational enlightenment and faith are in a kind of unchallenged dialectical collusion: in elevating God into a beyond—and the beyond need not simply be "up there"—faith is slowly divested of any claim to rational content, or indeed to any claim to rational consideration. The collusion of faith and Enlightenment that lives and lets live is really a remote death warrant for the seriousness of the religious. It may take some centuries for the death warrant to take effect, but the slow bleeding has begun, and by now the patient has basically gotten used to its enfeebled condition, though it says it feels just fine. Faith comes to share in the absence of the essential, even though, like Enlightenment, it is also a protest against the prevailing ethos of alienation. But both protests against the absence of the essential are themselves complementary forms of the presence of this absence!

Beyond the self-knowledge of this condition, Heyde offers a very thoughtful reconstruction of some of the traditional ways to God, touching on the major "proofs" as articulated by Anselm, Aquinas, Descartes. What is distinctive here is the emphasis Heyde puts on what he terms *fundamental thought experiences (fundamentale denkervaringen)*. This important point here relates specifically to the engagement of the philosopher: there are experiences of thought that are not the empirical experiences that we know from sound common-sense perception, nor the methodologically reconstructed experience of concern in scientific experiment, but processes of undergoing that are peculiar to different configurations of philosophical thought on the question of God. These reveal their own inner exigencies that bring us in the direction of the affirmation of God.

Put otherwise: philosophy does not deal extrinsically with the question of God, as if the religious had a monopoly on the matter. There are no monopolies in relation to God, be they religious or not. Nor is it sufficient to rest with the simple opposition of the God of the philosophers and the God of Abraham, Isaac, and Jacob. A sympathetic hermeneutic of the nature of philosophical thought as experienced from within shows, so to say, a piety of thinking, and this not in any Heideggerian sense. Quite the contrary, one of the challenges of Heyde's discussion makes one rethink the inner riches of traditional orientations, forcing one to ask: Do many of current characterizations of these orientations, at times, verge of being a variety of philosophical cartoon? Heyde's portraits are far more faithful and persuasive.

The many strands in Kant's complex views are unpacked with admirable patience and clarity. Heyde reminds us that to see Kant univocally as the destroyer of metaphysics is a serious oversimplification. Quite to the contrary, what is barred in one direction, is reopened in another. The claim is made that the second direction is the better for human beings who would be honest about our essential finitude. Hegel is of aid again, with the dialectic of limit. We cannot absolutize finitude, for to think finitude at all necessarily means its surpassing, in the invocation of its other, the infinite. The thought that is truer to our self-surpassing process of moving to a limit must include reference to both sides. The Kantian project of drawing limits suffers from a dialectical equivocity: it presuppose something of what it ostensibly denies. Kant himself proceeds ambiguously to fill the breach of his first effort at critique by a second moral way—itself not void of dialectical equivocities.

One of the great enigmas of our finitude is our exposure to evil and Heyde does not avoid that exposure. Without backing away from the existential and moral horrors of evil, one might say that he gives an eloquent exegesis of Aquinas's terse statement: *Si malum est, Deus est*: if evil is, God is. He musters resources of thought from a variety of sources, philosophical and nonphilosophical. The intent is: neither to dispense with God because of evil, nor to obscure evil for the sake of God. While denying that evil is absolute, he makes no claim to domesticate conceptually its enigmatic recalcitrance.

Heyde's book is singularly lacking in gestures of dismissal. He concludes with reflections on Heidegger and Nietzsche as philosophers of finitude without relief. The so-called affirmation of finitude in Nietzsche and Heidegger does not escape an unstable equivocity, an equivocity not helped by the lapse into silence about the issue of God to which their thinking has differently contributed. By means of his rethinking of some older ways Heyde has already brought us to a dialectic of limit and openness. Now from another angle the suggestion is explored that a fully articulated *affirmation* of human finitude makes no sense without reference to the other of that finitude. God is not a flight from finitude but emerges in the most thoroughgoing thinking of its meaning. Not: because finitude no transcendence. But rather: without transcendence, no proper affirmation of finitude.

Heyde is most overtly sympathetic to Hegel. One suspects on occasion that the care, thoughtfulness, and thoroughness that mark his reconstruction, say, of Aquinas's ways and Anselm's, indicate something exceeding Hegel himself. Something of the air of transcendence as other breathes in these reconstructions: transcendence as other that is not always easy to reconcile with Hegel's dialectical way of thinking transcendence, with its seemingly inevitable drift to subordinating transcendence to a more fulfilled immanence. I say this not in criticism. There is more to what Heyde wants to say than Hegel's help always allows, but that more is just what we must try to think, and toward which Heyde points.

The book is a carefully crafted work, elegantly written in the original Dutch, with a nicely orchestrated development. Heyde reenacts for the reader something of the *passage of thought itself*, thought as experienced from within, rather than reported on simply from without. Such is the type of exploration needed to refresh our astonishment about the divine, and to awaken our philosophical perplexity about that most enigmatic and momentous of all questions. It is a boon to have this work now available in English, and not only for Hegel scholars, or philosophers interested in classical and contemporary responses to God, but for mindful human beings still wondering if we have wings.

Preface

To write about God is a perilous undertaking. On the one hand, we feel we say more than is possible. On the other hand, what we write can only lag behind the wealth and depth of a long philosophical tradition. Why then write? What could be the motive? In this book, it is the *wondering* about God's relative absence in contemporary philosophy, as well as the puzzling lack of interest in God displayed by our culture.

It is impossible to remove oneself from one's time, and thus to be completely freed from all it presupposes. Should we succeed in doing so, we would no longer be able to think. We are not granted complete insight into why we now think as we do. We can only try to stand back from what is prevalent. Is this not a minimal prerequisite of the search for understanding? The following is a venture in that direction. The matter is worked out through the development of certain experiences that thinking can pass through when it goes to its outermost limits, and there poses to itself the question concerning the ground of all that is.

This attempt would not have been possible without the help of others. I think of the many useful suggestions of my colleagues, of the care of Jeannine van Dyck, Riny Rijnders, and Anja de Jong in preparing the text for publication, and of the critical openness with which my students in Nijmegen approached the preliminary drafts during my lectures.

A special word of thanks on the occasion of the publication of the English version to the editorial staff of SUNY Press in New York and Boom in Amsterdam who made this publication possible. Also to Alexander Harmsen and William Desmond. Alex Harmsen prepared the basic translation. I thank him for the professional style in which he did it and for the friendly cooperation. My colleague and friend William Desmond corrected this first version of the translation and helped me with many suggestions. Only after the publication of the Dutch version of my book have I had the opportunity to study Desmond's work more fundamentally. Previously I knew him mainly from his book on Hegel's aesthetics. Thus, it was too late to incorporate the rich and original insights he has worked out in many other publications. I hope to do this in the future in other publications. With all diversity, there is a deep common philosophical orientation between us. I thank him for his support, his willingness to risk the "adventure" of an English edition of my book, and for his willingness to write a foreword.

Introduction

The time of militant atheism seems far behind us. Few are now gripped by Sartre's passionate display, when he defended the view that human freedom and acceptance of God were mutually exclusive. "We live in a time after the death of God"—the slogan functioned as self evident. The thought he voices barely holds the dramatic tension surrounding it in the work of Nietzsche.

Even fewer seem moved by such themes as "faith and world," "reason and faith," "belief in God and human responsibility." Such themes seem to have lost not only their existential but also their intellectual impact. Except perhaps in enclaves that seem to shrink continuously, God seems to have gradually disappeared in the folds of history. Of course, there are still churches, believers, different forms of religiosity, devout people, theological texts, texts on philosophy of religion. Nevertheless—and my point relates to the postindustrial Euro-American world—conviction about God no longer plays a dynamic role in our culture. It no longer elicits great intellectual debates. It seems hard put to evince any spirit of passion.

God seems to wither in a growing lack of interest.

The following chapters have their source in a feeling of wonder about the unbelievable "erosion of the supreme being,"[1] about the fact that God no longer seems to inspire interest. My concerns in this study, therefore, are philosophical in nature. How is it possible that the very thing that had played such a dominant role in the history of Western metaphysics now seems drained of interest? How are we to understand this marginalization of what once provoked intense, fundamental, and closely argued thinking, what once was the central organizing point of brilliant philosophical discourse?

Does it mean that thought has finally matured enough to put things in the balance, and in all lucidity decide no longer to occupy itself with what seems beyond the reach of reason? Or is all philosophical concern with God a concealed form of theology, or merely an affair of personal faith? Has God become of interest only to the private life of an individual? Is God too esoteric for the "enlightened" mind and thus not the proper concern of philosophy? Or is something much more fundamental at stake? Do we deal with something to which philosophical reason itself lacks access, something which comes over it, a fate that strikes it, a *Geschick*[2] through which reality appears solely in the light of a radical finitude? Or has it nothing to do with thinking, reasoning, argumentation, proof, and construction, but with something that lies deeper: feelings, moods, experiences, all the forms of our prereflexive relation with actuality? Is that not what is insinuated by the word disinterest: something has ceased to speak to us, to move us?

Wonder, the beginning of all philosophy, is in no way the cosseting of one's ignorance. Wonder only comes to those who desire to *understand*. Aristotle has clearly shown us that wonder contains its inherent dynamic to bring us to understanding.[3] Yet how are we to come to insight concerning the perplexing "disappearance" of God from philosophical discourse? What is this disappearance? What is it that disappears? Who or what is the "God of the philosophers"?

There is no special method to guarantee us a "solution" to all these questions. No well-trodden paths lie open, placing before us the gaining of our goal. One can only try, and see whether one comes any closer to the issue provoking and motivating us. This will not be a regal exposition of the truth, but rather a venture on the road toward the truth.

We are not the first to attempt such an undertaking. For this reason this book often makes reference to the tradition and the *experiences of thought* in which it is rooted.[4] This tradition is not entirely alien to us. If we let the tradition tell its own story, we will hear the history of our own becoming. We cannot understand ourselves and what awakens our wonder without undertaking a crucial detour. This detour is very remarkable. Far from leading away from our goal, it is rather the prerequisite for reaching it. If one cannot grant the time for such a detour, or bear the burden of the delay, one will never arrive at the issue at hand. Haste is the great enemy of thought.

It is not easy to let oneself be genuinely affected by the issue, and to stand open before the many experiences of thought it has elicited. This presupposes that one ceases to take for granted, or suspend one's absorption in, the ruling culture, refusing to be dragged along by prevailing fashion. This is not easy for then one may have the experience of being deprived of what makes one feel at home, indeed comfortable. Mostly we resist confrontation with the truth of our situation and the world. This is brilliantly displayed in Plato's allegory of the Cave and in Hegel's *Phenomenology of Spirit*.

If we want to approach the matter in question, namely God, and if we want to assume an authentic and free relation toward it, then a *conditio sine qua non* is the critique of the preconceptions and opinions we ordinarily take as self-evident. Such a critique opens a space wherein one can approach the problem of God with renewed freedom.

Naturally such a critique of experience cannot start from nothing: where there is nothing, nothing begins. It requires a challenge, an impulse, a confrontation with other experiences and thoughts. Critique is another word for the difficult and patient practice of a thinking that does not grant itself comfort. It demands that one's thinking seeks to move toward its utmost possibilities. Such a critique, however, knows how to guard itself against the failure that is due to its fear of error.[5] This occurs when thinking loses its hospitable regard for the other, the strange, the unthought, the unexpected. This happens when the longing for personal certainty so overcomes us that reality is not allowed to reveal itself as it is, with all the references it bears within itself.

To philosophize is to attempt to take hold of the *tension* between *critique* and *openness*. It presupposes a methodological caution about our every word, experience, and theory, as well as an absolute receptivity to all that we witness, all thought and every explanation. It can only succeed when one is gripped by a demand for *truth* and *actuality*. Herein lies the only passion that philosophy permits itself.

This is not a passion that paralyzes thought, nor a power that scatters or obscures it. On the contrary, it is *a desire* that drives thinking forward and prevents it from taking up residence in half-truths or easy self-evidences. Where philosophy strives to its outermost limit, and would measure itself against the question of God, this desire is put to its severest test. Thus, Kant warned that theoretical reason here acknowledges something that exceeds its possibilities. Does it not then leave the safe "island" of truth tested by experience? Does it not, as he puts it, lose itself in a "wide and stormy ocean, the native home of illusion, where many a fog bank and many a swiftly melting iceberg give the deceptive appearance of farther shores, deluding the adventurous seafarer ever anew with empty hopes, and engaging him in enterprises which he can never abandon and yet is unable to carry to completion"?[6]

Must we in philosophy not lay to rest the question of God, and hand it over to religion, or the sphere of mere subjective conviction, where many think it belongs? Does not reason and intellectual integrity demand "silence concerning that whereof we cannot speak"? Modesty can be charming but in itself it is no guarantee of truth. He who banishes the question of God from philosophy does not know more about the possibilities and limits of thought than he who deals with it. He only knows differently. It is premature to come to a decision on this, before having tried the road toward clarification of the problematic itself.

As I said earlier, there is no royal road that leads us there. There are only many ways, paths, some of them roundabout. There are no *summas* but rather some ventures of thought.

A first venture concerns the *puzzling loss of interest* displayed in the problematic of God in contemporary culture, and especially in philosophy.

This venture—constituting the first chapter—is a detour needed to ease our entry into a fuller unfolding of the question of God in the chapters that follow. I am concerned to clarify a particular *understanding of actuality* that to a large extent dominates our culture. It affects how we understand God, but it is not always explicit. It works in diverse ways and assumes many forms. It does not coincide with

4

any particular theory or explicit ideology, but lies deeper. It functions on a level that is determinative for many different ideas, theories, orientations, and convictions. Our thinking cannot sovereignly make it entirely manifest; for it seems already to regulate our thinking. Hegel's remark concerning philosophy—namely, that it is the child of its time—undoubtedly holds for the entire ensemble of ideas, opinions, prejudices, and experiences that determine thought in a multiplicity of ways. It is almost trivial to put forward the argument that not only our ideas, but also our experiences of humankind and world are characterized by historicity. This also holds for contemporary ideas and "experiences" of God. Of these the human being is not, without further ado, the simple author. People usually ascertain, with more or less wonder, that actuality appears as it does and not in another way.

To penetrate to the roots and clarify this dominant understanding is an almost hopeless task. We can, however, try to piece together the flotsam and jetsam that we gather. Perhaps we can bring to light a particular logic that makes the dominant understanding intelligible, at least to some degree.

How to begin this detour? How break through to that understanding that hiddenly dominates our thinking about God? The chapter now to follow must be read both as a *hypothesis* and, in a certain sense, as a *proposal*.

A *hypothesis*: the view developed is that the dominant understanding of reality, relative to the question of God, has its roots in the Enlightenment. More precisely formulated: what announces itself in the Enlightenment has *now* attained its full realization. With regard to the philosophical problematic of God, the now dominant logic receives its initial form in the Enlightenment.

In that respect, modernity, in fact, dominates that culture often presented as postmodern. But what is the Enlightenment? Is there such a thing at all? Every interpretation of the Enlightenment gives form to what we have come to consider as an independent reality— namely, the Enlightenment itself. The interpretation of the Enlightenment is co-constitutive of its essence. This does not mean we can arbitrarily move in any direction: creative interpretation does not simply create the matter with which it is involved.

5

On this question of interpretation, my hypothesis is bound up with a *proposal*. The key to the dominant understanding is not to be sought in the Enlightenment as such (what would that be?), but in Hegel's interpretation of it—namely, as found in his *Phenomenology of Spirit*. My proposal is to decipher the specific logic of the dominant understanding by way of Hegel's account of the Enlightenment.

This does not mean that Hegel's account is an "explanation" of dominant ways of thinking. Nor that the Enlightenment is the "cause" of contemporary thinking and experience. Hegel's interpretation functions rather as a *hermeneutical key*, allowing us access to what implicitly governs current thought about God. Our concern is thus not simply an analysis of the Enlightenment, nor an exhaustive exegesis of Hegel or his interpretation of the Enlightenment. My concern is with our own culture, and especially, the puzzling lack of interest in the problem of God, which awakens our wonder. My concern is the basic conception of actuality that governs our experience, speech, and thought about God. Hegel's elucidation is a detour that can help us see through what seems self-evident to our culture and simply taken for granted.

What dominates—as shall be shown—is a certain *logic of absence*. The absolute, God, is understood as that which is not present. This understanding of God does not stand on its own. *Theology*[7] is included in a much broader logic that itself implicates an *ontology* as well as an *anthropology*. Hegel's account is extraordinarily fruitful precisely to unveil the interwovenness of theology, ontology, and anthropology. Otherwise formulated: Hegel's interpretation of the Enlightenment gives us a direction concerning this interwovenness, putting us in a position to see with new eyes what we are and think.

Theology, ontology, and anthropology come into contact with each other at a point which, historically speaking, initially takes shape in the Enlightenment, and is now dominant in thinking about God—namely, the idea: *what is present is not essential, and what is essential is not present*.[8]

The first chapter attempts to clarify this thesis. If my hypothesis succeeds and the reader accepts the proposal, nothing will be "explained." At most, what is now dominant will be revealed: a certain

6

configuration of consciousness, a *particular* understanding of one's ownmost "I," the world, and the absolute. In this way, what *now* happens to hold loses the absolute status it has when taken as something self-evident.

Thus arises a clearing and an openness, both conditions for a *free engagement* with the experiences of thought in philosophy that lead to the affirmation of God. These experiences will be described and partially reconstructed in the *second* and *third* chapters.

Also in chapter *three* and subsequently in chapter *four*, we will explore in what measure such experiences of thought can maintain their genuine standing over against other kinds of experiences. The *first* is of a theoretical nature, and concerns the limits of thought. The *second* is existential and moral, and engages the experience of suffering and evil.

In the *concluding chapter* a balance is drawn up. In a confrontation with Heidegger and Nietzsche, I attempt to come to an appreciation of *finitude* that, although radical, embraces the affirmation of God.

1

The Absence of the Essential

However original and powerful thought may be, it cannot completely avoid the grip of tradition, of context, of the *Zeitgeist*, of one or more paradigms or ruling ideas. There is no Archimedean point upon which we can sovereignly build our own thought. Thought does not just appear in history, it is steeped in historicity. The power of original thinking manifests itself within *history* and not in a vacuum.

The dream of every philosophy "to begin completely anew from the ground up" therefore presupposes an "undoing of all opinions thus far received."[1] One must well understand Descartes, whom I paraphrase here. He does not plead for a sort of absolute nullpoint from which to undertake a thinking without any determinacy, much less without the elementary laws of logic. At stake is the undoing of *opinions*. This does not require we seek a point outside history from where, as a sort of "conscience survolante," one can survey everything. "The undoing of all received opinions" entails breaking through the self-evident influence of all kinds of conceptions, rather than the undoing of history. The latter is not only an illusion. Were it to be realizable, the destruction of one's own thought would follow. What determines us in various ways, our prejudices, are also the conditions of possibility for independent thought. Breaking through the self-evident entails coming to an understanding of the history in which one assumes a position, and of its operative ideas.

To think originally about God in "the time after the death of God"—a paradoxical venture indeed—requires coming to grips with the complex logic currently dominant. In the introduction I called this the *logic of absence*. This logic includes a multiplicity of different ideas that yet are related to one another, reciprocally strengthen each other, and come together at one central point—namely, *that the essential is absent.*

This logic has a tripartite structure. First, it encompasses a specific *theology*. God is understood as a beyond (*Jenseits*), on the other side of *this* world, as an abstract being, a vague hypothetical principle, or as indeterminate transcendence and not as the ground of the actuality wherein we live. Second, this theology corresponds to a certain *ontology* (or *cosmology*) in which nothing offered to us by the world of experience can be considered as essential. Nothing of what is turns out to be substantial. Third, the nihilistic logic in which thinking about God and world mirror each other, encompasses a particular *anthropology*. The latter is anthropocentric in nature: the human being is the ultimate reference point of all meaning. At first sight it seems that the idea of absence is not relevant here. Is the human for itself not here the essential reality? In the concrete analysis that follows, it will become clear that this is not the case: the human subject itself is ultimately substanceless and contaminated by the loss of the essential.

As indicated, this logic undergoes a concretization and a historical embodiment in Hegel's interpretation of the Enlightenment, specifically in the crusade of enlightened reason against faith. In the following sections I reconstruct some important elements of this struggle. My concern is, as I have said, not with the historical context but with the particular *Gestalt* or *form of consciousness* taking shape therein. Formulated differently: Hegel's analysis functions as a *hermeneutical model* or as a kind of *mirror* that can foster a reflexive consciousness of what dominates in our culture. Obviously, the logic manifest in it can only be clarified when also the historical "story" is told. Once again, however, this last point is not my primary concern.[2]

1.1 An Essenceless World

Hegel's interpretation of the Enlightenment brings together a multiplicity of motives. One is the struggle between *reason* liberating itself from all servitude and what Hegel calls *faith*. Faith is not to be identified simply with religion or Christian faith. It concerns a *particular Gestalt* of Christian religion. Hegel characterizes this in the context of seventeenth- and eighteenth-century Europe, but it also serves the function of an ideal type. This is likewise the case with the Enlightenment, which, among other things, is presented as a reaction to such faith. Faith and Enlightenment each represent a particular understanding of the human being, world, and God.

They have a sense that surpasses the seventeenth and eighteenth century, in the way that, for example, Greek democracy has a political meaning that reaches beyond its time. That meaning does not coincide with the historical conditions of its appearance in the Greek city states of the fifth century before Christ. Hegel's *Phenomenology* is not any ordinary historiography of Western European humanity. It is more a typology, partially projected into history, of ways in which we can understand ourselves and our world.[3] Faith and Enlightenment are forms of such an understanding.

Faith arises in a particular cultural context. That is, the social and political world is experienced as something in which the free spirit cannot be at home with itself. It is estranged from its essence. Faith is the movement of searching in "an other world" for what one's own reality no longer offers. What then is the status of the world where the spirit is alienated from itself? What kind of world is this?[4]

Historically it concerns prerevolutionary Europe, specifically the French world of the seventeenth and eighteenth century. This is a world both socially divided and economically and politically marked by great instability. This instability also expresses itself in moral experience. It is a world in which firm values are devalued and established moral relations are dismantled. The stability of feudal society is dissolved in a culture in which political power and wealth become the highest values. Society hereby enters into a vortex where nothing is secure and everything constantly changes or is other than it seems. Everything appears to be *vain*. Nothing substantial remains. This is not only our perspective, as we view that world retrospectively, and from without. The awareness of vanity also marks the consciousness of those who do everything to acquire political power or wealth: they know that what they pursue and

11

seize is ultimately vain. This unstable, vain, all-perverting world is also thus a cynical world.

Diderot's novel *Le Neveu de Rameau* is an exemplary expression of this state of mind. What everyone knows but is barely stated, is here expressed openly and frankly: all is vain. The world seems to have lost its essence. The spirit is thus estranged from itself: actuality is no longer the other in which the spirit can be at home with itself.

This essencelessness can be illustrated in various ways.

The Reversal of Positions—First of all this becomes apparent in the complete shift in the types of consciousness dominant in the world, and in the disappearance of the firm difference that keeps them separate. In modern times the individual is no longer harmoniously encompassed by the life of the community. The beautiful harmony of Greek ethical life lies far behind us. The community is experienced as external to the individual. Its harmony shatters into differentiated spheres which answer to different powers.

On the one hand, there is the power of the state. This represents the universal over against the multitude of particular individuals. On the other hand, there is the realm of wealth: the economic life of a people. Here the particular prevails, although not exclusively. For the interplay of the many particular interests is determined by general laws that govern economic life.

Each of these two powers can be valued in different ways. So the power of the state appears as something good in so far as it represents the universality of the particular individuals, but it appears as something bad as far as it demands subjugation. Wealth is something good in so far as it is the expression of individual freedom, but it is bad as the source of inequality, egoism, as something that places individuals in opposition to each other.

Correlative with these various evaluations are different types of consciousness. Hegel distinguishes between a noble and a base consciousness (*das edelmütige Bewusstsein, das niederträchtige Bewusstsein*).[5]

The noble consciousness is a positive consciousness. It serves the power of the state and realizes itself in unity with the universal.

It is grateful for wealth. It considers wealth as the realization of the particular side of its being. Historically we recognize here the attitude that typifies the pre-Revolutionary aristocracy. By contrast, the base or ignoble consciousness comports itself in a negative manner toward both powers. It accepts the power of the state because it cannot do otherwise. The universality of the state is experienced as something that oppresses the individual. That is why subjugation is accompanied by a feeling of rebelliousness. On the one hand, the base consciousness searches for wealth; on the other, he despises it because it merely offers the realization of the external side of his existence, it cannot completely fulfill his being.

However, any fixed distinction between these two forms of consciousness is a mere illusion. In concrete social life the positions pass over into each other. The noble consciousness ultimately turns out to be base, and the truth of the state's power turns out to be wealth. With this dialectical movement Hegel voices the principles that are decisive in the rise of the absolute monarchy and the pre-Revolutionary situation that goes with it.

The noble consciousness witnesses the satisfaction of its particularity in heroic service to the universality of the state. The detachment from private objectives that such service requires provides its own kind of satisfaction that lies in honor and a feeling of self-worth. But this detachment and honor turn out be somewhat ambiguous. When this dedication to the universal fails to result in a heroic sacrifice on the battlefield, it becomes more and more an instrument for the satisfaction of individual interests.

This is primarily visible in the institution of the court. When the noble becomes a courtier—and this is essential in the constitution of the absolute monarchy—the universal is reduced to an instrument for the promotion of private interests. To that end the noble alienates his innermost self. He lowers himself to the status of mere ornament around the throne of the monarch. This loss of self finds expression in the perversion of the language. His counsel degenerates into flattery: speech whose only function is constantly to tell the addressed what he is—absolute monarch. The noble thus trades his honor in return for material gain and privileges. He has now become a base consciousness which seeks wealth at all costs.

With this reversal the nature of state power also alters. It becomes a mere show that hides the real power: wealth.

The Dominion of Wealth—Here the world's lack of the essential becomes apparent in a second way. The power of the state represented the universality of the life of a community. This now appears as being completely emptied and turns over into its opposite, wealth. This means that the free ethical substance falls prey to the power of the particular and thus is lost. When wealth becomes the absolute, social life disintegrates into a multiplicity of oppositions and inequities. Excessive disparities arise between rich and poor. This alienation of the community is mirrored in an alienation of the individual. The self is "reified":—self-realization ends up being reduced to the world of "things"—money and possessions. At the same time the self abandons its autonomy: via wealth it becomes dependent on others. In place of respect and gratitude for the benefits of wealth, there arise feelings of dependency and hate. For the self knows that it is dependent on an alien will, on the whims and arbitrary will of an other.

Comedy and Cynicism—This is beautifully illustrated in Diderot's *Le Neveu de Rameau*. Hegel interprets the dialogue between the nephew of the famous composer and the philosopher Diderot as an expression of the essenceless world that will go under in the Revolution. *Nevertheless there is something universal in the text.* There is a model for a world—regardless of any historical period—whose substantial content has become problematic; a world subject to a permanent *dislocation* of positions and *inversion* of established values. Therefore the philosopher (Diderot) is led into confusion by the bohemian (Rameau's nephew). With his cynical speech the latter throws the firm determinations belonging to the former's world into disorder. Yet the bohemian simply allows us to see what is, in fact, the case. He says what everyone thinks, but that most dare not say—namely, that behind all honor, virtue, generosity, and honesty hides an ordinary reality: the power of money and the arrogance of wealth. This total perversion is given form in the conduct and language of the bohemian. Time and again he is other than what people think.

He continually plays different roles. He is this whirling succession of roles. He is a curious mixture of nobility and ordinary vulgarity, of high-mindedness and cynical calculation. He humiliates himself, but does so in a comical way, such that he is able to retain some dignity. In a certain sense he raises himself above the emptiness and baseness of his time through the honesty with which he expresses what others do and think. Does he acquire a substantial form in this way? Surely not, because the vanity of everything also contaminates his innermost self: it is no more than a set of roles in the general societal comedy.

Le neveu de Rameau can be read as a *postmodern* text avant-la-lettre. This is brilliantly expressed in the passage of Diderot's text which Hegel himself cites. Hegel writes: 'The content of what the spirit says about itself is thus the perversion of every notion and reality, the universal deception of itself and others; and the shamelessness which gives utterance to this deception is just for that reason the greatest truth." This kind of talk, says Hegel, is the madness (*Verrücktheit*) of the musician who (here Hegel cites Diderot) "leaped up and mixed together thirty arias, Italian, French, tragic, comic, of every sort; now with a deep basis he descended into hell, then, contracting his throat, he rent vaults of heaven with a falsetto tone, frantic and soothed, imperious and mocking, by turns."

To the tranquil consciousness which, in its honest way, takes the melody of the Good and the True to consist in the evenness of the notes—that is, in unison—this talk appears, as expressed now again by Diderot, as a "rigmarole of wisdom and folly, as a medley of as much skill as baseness, of as many correct as false ideas, a mixture compounded of a complete perversion of sentiment, of absolute shamefulness, and of perfect frankness and truth."[6]

1.2 THE PROTEST OF FAITH

Nothing essential is present in this torn and alienating world. It calls forth a particular religious consciousness that Hegel refers to as *faith* (*Glaube*). To the implicit ontology and anthropology corresponds a specific *theology*: a certain insight into what God is. This particular religious consciousness turns out to be internally marked by the same essencelessness against which it opposes itself. Faith initially manifests itself as a *flight* from the actual world. The spirit no longer finds satisfaction in it and thus turns to another world. This other, "unreal" world is termed by Hegel the world of *"pure consciousness,"* that is, a consciousness untainted by its entanglement in this world. This unreal world takes on two forms. On the one hand, it presents itself as *faith*, as consciousness of the spiritual essence. On the other hand, it is *pure insight*, the movement of the self that, all-knowing and criticizing all, denies every alterity, dissolving every object through the power of the thinking self.

The world of pure insight will manifest itself historically as the *Enlightenment*. Among other things it will be characterized by its opposition to the other form of pure consciousness—namely, faith. I will say more about this later. We are, after all, not following the development of Hegel's thought in detail. We are concerned with the development of a certain form of relation to the absolute. In doing so we are guided by Hegel's views on faith and the motif of absence connected with it.

That faith, just like the world to which it opposes itself, is marked by the absence of the essential. It seems strange at first sight. Is faith not the firm conviction in a divine world that is revealed in the Christian religion?[7] Is this divine world not *the* essence, in the light of which this world cannot really be considered as real? Does devotion, the service and the worship belonging to religious praxis, not exist in order to ensure a union with God, in order to give oneself to this other world? Even though it is not real in the same sense as is *this* world *here*, it is nonetheless real in a specific sense—it is the "true actuality" itself. Must faith not be understood as the presentation of something that is real and substantial in a cynical world without certainty? Although faith is all of these things, upon closer inspection it seems that it takes part in a remarkable way in the very world from which it wants to retreat. Its "theology" correlates with an implicit ontology and anthropology. Further analysis of the distinguishing characteristics of faith will clarify this.[8]

Faith as Flight—Faith is a protest against the essencelessness of actuality. It flees from it and says that the genuine reality is *elsewhere*, on the other side of this reality in a world which is merely *thought*— better formulated, a world merely *represented*. This other world is the immediate opposite of this world. Nevertheless, this form of opposition carries with it the idea that the *negation* of this world is, at the same time, a certain *affirmation* of it. Faith does not change this world. On the contrary, it is precisely by virtue of the flight from this lack of the essential that this world receives something irreducible. In this way the purity of the flight from the world is tainted. In various ways the *essenceless* actuality continues to play an active role in the nonactual essentiality.

The one consciousness constantly lives in two worlds. A substantial part of its existence is subject to a world that it denies from the point of view of faith. Furthermore, the purity of the *beyond* is repeatedly violated by various anthropomorphisms which faith utilizes in order to denote its object. The content of faith is presented as a whole of contingent happenings, as a history of salvation. As a *history* of salvation, nature is repeated on a supernatural level, though under an altered sign. Although faith knows that what is referred to in various signs such as bread and wine is something "beyond," the materiality of the symbols contaminates the purity of its principles.

The essenceless world continues to play a role and remains present in the asceticism, the service, and worship through which believers indeed realize their union with the essential. The earthly reality is merely renounced in a symbolic manner, so that this negation is at the same time an affirmation. That from which we free ourselves is so trivial that its occurrence could be at most of token value. Thus symbolic renunciation can easily function as an alibi for a complete surrender to "earthly goods" outside of worship. To this remarkable dialectic, whereby that which is denied—precisely because the denial is immediate—is affirmed, we will later return when discussing the critique of the Enlightenment.

The Essencelessness of Faith—Faith is not just a protest against the absence of the essential; it is itself internally characterized by absence. This primarily comes to the fore in the logic that determines its religious attitude. The terms with which Hegel characterizes faith point predominantly to the *logic of essence*. In the second part of the *Science of Logic* those categories of thought are developed that we employ when we take reality not as something immediate, but rather as the appearance of something else that is called essential. Here thought works with categories such as essence and appearance, cause and effect, substance and accident, matter and form, law and instance, exteriority and interiority. This is the sphere of relation and reflection. Here all determinations point to each other, mirror each other, without the unifying ground that makes all these reflections possible being thought. Thought runs aground on correlations and dualities. In phenomenological terms one could describe this sphere as the sphere of *alienation* in which the idea is estranged from the fundamental unity that it is in-itself.

Faith operates within this logic. It understands its object (God, the absolute) as *mere essence* in opposition to immediate actuality. The absolute is thought of as purely in-itself, as alienated from existence, as simple interiority, as mere positive in absolute equality with itself, as self-sufficient and in absolute rest. In relation to its "object," of course, faith distinguishes between the intratrinitarian moments and the economy of salvation as made up of creation, incarnation, and return to unity with the Father. However, due to the representational form inherent in faith, it is not adequate to think its fundamental unity with its object. Faith conceives "its" absolute as elsewhere and not as present here and now: it understands it only as essence and not as spiritual actuality.

Furthermore, absence dominates in another manner—namely, in the continuation of the previous manner. God is not only absent because God is "elsewhere," but also because God surpasses any and all insight. Faith is caught in an opposition of consciousness in which an insurmountable gap exists between self-consciousness and its object. The supernatural world of God is wholly other to self-consciousness and so "the essence of faith is no longer a [pure] thought, but is reduced to the level of something represented, and becomes a supersensible world which is essentially an other in relation to self-consciousness."[9] Faith turns out to be the affirmation of a content that retreats from intellectual understanding.

Thus it is a matter of necessity that there is an unrelenting struggle between *uninsightful faith* and *unfaithful insight*, between faith and pure insight. This conflict is not bound to the historical context in which Hegel discusses it. It has a structural necessity: *where humankind thinks this way about God, this conflict must present itself.* This does not apply exclusively to the Enlightenment. More precisely: it applies to every understanding of God that moves within the frame of reference that became dominant in the Enlightenment. Perhaps—and this is my hypothesis—the essential characteristics of this frame of reference are still dominant in our culture. The hard core of this frame of reference is what I have called the *logic of absence*, a logic that expresses itself in an ontology, an anthropology, and a theology. An *ontology*: nothing is essential, everything is reduced to utility. An *anthropology*: the human being is central as an indifferent user or consumer. A *theology*: God is understood as absent, as elsewhere, and as an indeterminate, empty transcendence. This will all become more clear once faith has adapted itself to the critique levied against it by the Enlightenment. Then God will not just be elsewhere, as is the case now, God will also dissolve in empty abstractions.

This configuration represents a framework of thought that *blocks philosophical ways of thinking about God and leads our relation with the tradition into misunderstanding*, provided that the self-evident workings of this logic remain unexposed. Then this configuration reigns as a fate which deprives thought of its *freedom*.

If we succeed in breaking through this *forgetfulness*—the main issue of this chapter—then we have not yet found the way to God. On the contrary, at this point *everything is still* open. It is this openness that concerns us. It prepares thought for a *free relationship* with experiences of thought wherein God is affirmed. What thinking then decides, in this free relationship, is a further matter.

The aim of the rest of this chapter is a more detailed clarification of this logic.

1.3 THE "RETRIEVAL" OF THE ESSENTIAL
THE STRUGGLE OF THE ENLIGHTENMENT

The Enlightenment is not only a critical movement opposed to forms of belief. It is also, in the first place, like faith itself, a critique of the various forms of alienation that appear in the culture. Faith demonstrated the vanity of the world through focusing on a being that is *beyond*, on a genuine *content*. In the critique put forth by the Enlightenment the *form* stands central. The spirit elevates itself above the actual, not so much by virtue of one or another content, but through the activity of critical thought itself. Not *what* is thought but *that* one thinks, that everything is subject to the norm of critical reason, that the self and *its own insight* are ultimate—these are what characterize the Enlightenment. In a variation on Kant's celebrated *Wahlspruch*, Hegel says, "This pure insight is thus the Spirit that calls to every consciousness: *be for* yourselves what you all are *in yourselves—reasonable*."[10] That is why the Enlightenment aspires to remove the positivity from all *given* content and thereby reduce it to the concept. What is at stake is the right to one's own insight and the active negativity of self-consciousness.

From Hegel's speculative conception, the struggle of the Enlightenment with faith is understood as the battle in which the spirit engages with itself. In the object of its criticism the Enlightenment strikes itself. In the object of faith reason represents itself in an unconscious manner such that faith becomes the expression of self-consciousness (this will later be decisive in Feuerbach's interpretation of religion.) All this, however, is only clear for us who philosophize and attempt to understand the entire situation retrospectively. Initially the truth of the matter is hidden for the explicit self-consciousness of enlightened reason. With this last point I concern myself now.

God's Disappearance—For the Enlightenment faith is simply other, the opposite of reason and truth. It is a web of superstition, prejudices, and errors.[11] It exists only due to a peculiar interplay of the many, the priests and a despot. The deceit and the cynicism of the priests (who know better!) only succeed due to the deficiency of spiritual power of the masses. This whole is reinforced and maintained by the despot. He uses the stupidity of the masses and the mendacity of the priesthood to his own advantage and in order to oppress his subjects.

The most decisive manner in which the Enlightenment wages its battle against faith is through a kind of all-encompassing corrosion of the opinions and attitudes of the masses. Against the mendacious consciousness of the priest it is unable to do anything immediately. Their cynicism makes them less vulnerable. The masses, by contrast, are more vulnerable. What the Enlightenment asserts is in principle not foreign to the people. The Enlightenment does nothing more than awaken the rationality and critical sense which lie as yet dormant. That is why it carries out its activity by way of a peaceful diffusion through the entire society. The mentality of the society changes gradually without any real opposition. The proliferation of the position of pure insight is, according to Hegel "comparable to a silent expansion or to the *diffusion*, say of a perfume in the unresisting atmosphere. It is a penetrating infection which does not make itself noticeable beforehand as something opposed to the indifferent element into which it insinuates itself, and *therefore cannot be warded off.*"[12]

Once the effects of this universal contamination become visible, it is too late for any remedy, because the Enlightenment appeals to the implicit inner essence of the initially uncultivated masses. That is why society was unable to fend off the movement of the Enlightenment. (However, the Enlightenment must be applied to itself.) This specific activity is evoked by Hegel in a pregnant manner with a further reference to *Le Neveu de Rameau*. The section in the *Phenomenology* reads: "Being now an invisible and imperceptible Spirit, it infiltrates the noble parts through and through and soon has taken complete possession of all the vitals and members of the unconscious idol." Then "One fine morning it gives its comrade a shove with the elbow, and bang! Crash! The idol lies on the floor."[13] With this allusion to the technique with which the Jesuits, according to Diderot, spread the Christian faith in China and India—without an uproar, without bloodshed, and without martyrs—he identifies the way in which the new God of reason dislodged all others. One fine day the people realized that they are no longer there. Through the silent activity of reason God has disappeared.

The "Unsatisfied Enlightenment"—Within the context of an almost natural spread of the Enlightenment there appears an explicit opposition to faith. The Enlightenment does not operate only as an invisible infection. It also takes the form of "a sheer uproar and a violent struggle."[14]

This struggle is filled with ambiguities. The Enlightenment reproaches faith for focusing on a strange actuality, on something irrational and contrary to all reasonable insight—a strange object, absolutely foreign to self-consciousness, and in an underhand way presented to consciousness by mendacious priests. The Enlightenment speaks of "priestly deception deluding the people . . . as if by some hocus-pocus of conjuring priests consciousness had been palmed off with something absolutely alien and "other" to it in the place of its own essence."[15] Nevertheless, the Enlightenment is inconsequential in its critique. When it declares the object of faith a fiction,[16] something brought forth by consciousness itself, it denies the very strangeness it had criticized in the first instance. A large part of the critique is a kind of "Feuerbachianism" *avant la lettre*. For it accentuates the identity of the religious consciousness and its object.

As we have seen, faith is not only contemplative (*credere Deum*).[17] It also has its own efficacy. Through service, asceticism, and worship, consciousness realizes its unity with the divine. Here it enacts the very principle of pure insight: making "for-itself" what was initially "in-itself." This being-for-itself and this unity with its object are apparent in the trust (*credere Deo*) that characterizes faith. This entails that faith in God is also experienced as the expression of subjective certainty.

The self finds itself again in God. Therefore it can deliver itself to God. God is *intimior intimo meo*. God is what is most intimate to the self. That is why faith is at the same time a consciousness of one's own infinitude. Feuerbach will later unilaterally emphasize this moment of unity with the divine being and this generation of the object of faith as something whose source lies in the self. He will present it as sufficient reason for faith and thus unmask faith as anthropomorphic. In this he continues the critique of the Enlightenment. Implied therein is that the unity characterizing trust, the very *product* of the object of faith, is unmoored from its *givenness,* so that faith is reduced to an artificial *fiction (Erdichtung)*. With this, however, the religious comportment is denatured. Faith knows that the activity of the self and the unity are only necessary and not sufficient conditions for the object. Moreover, in this way the essence of the givenness is misunderstood. It is reduced to an effect of the deceitful activity of the priests and thus to something that comes wholly from without.[18]

Yet this critique is nevertheless effective, notwithstanding all the misunderstandings and misconceptions it voices with respect to faith. It leads to a "deconstruction" of the immediate unity that marks faith in its simplicity.

The symbolization of the divine being in various signs, such as an image, a gesture, or a piece of bread becomes problematic. Through the mistrust and lack of understanding of the Enlightenment, the symbolic process no longer can fulfill its function. It is reduced to *superstition*. Faith is in part responsible for this turn of events because it is predominantly directed toward the absence of its object and thus cannot adequately conceive of its immanence. The unity of the divine and the human is impoverished to an external proximity of two spheres, to an "on the one hand" and an "on the other hand," to an "also."

In all this the symbolic process is reduced to an improper blend of the pure divine being with impure actuality. Faith loses its original open-mindedness. It becomes anxious about various forms of *anthropomorphism*. It flees from this danger by purifying God of all predicates (every predicate already bears an anthropomorphic, earthly connotation). God is reduced to an empty, indeterminate transcendence, an absolute being without predicates, unknown, and unrecognizable, something that can only be an object of infinite longing. Consequently faith becomes *nostalgia*.

The remarkable aspect of this "defensive" strategy of faith is that it draws faith in the direction of its opponent. Faith's view of God now scarcely differs from the deism of the Enlightenment. The only difference is that faith is unhappy with this result. It suffers from indeterminacy and the absence of what is essential; it becomes, as Hegel writes, an *unsatisfied Enlightenment* (*unbefriedigte Aufklärung*).[19]

The critique has rendered faith even more unreal than it already was in its immediate denial of the alienated culture. Not only the content of faith (namely, its conception of God), but also its epistemological foundations are "deconstructed" in the same way.

Originally faith was a simple unity of eternal truth and historical mediation (the idea of a "salvation history"). This unity is broken by the critique levied by enlightened reason. This critique operates primarily by way of the understanding (*Verstand*), which through its activity of separating and analyzing, time and again generates new distinctions and oppositions.[20] The critique reduces the foundation of faith to controversial historical facts, divorced from their deeper religious meaning. Because faith is imprisoned in the logic of absence, because it considers the essential to be absent, it is extremely susceptible to this critique. It succumbs to the deficient interpretation the Enlightenment presents and tries to prove its own truth with pure facts and sheer historical argumentation. It thus enters into the logic of its opponent. With this "adaptation" it prepares it own downfall.

1.4 A ONE-DIMENSIONAL WORLD AND A DISTANT GOD

Our main concern in this chapter has been the clarification of a certain logic: the logic of the absence of the essential. This logic has a tripartite structure. It links a theology, an ontology, and an anthropology. It functions as a *hermeneutical model* to unveil a dominant understanding of actuality in modern culture. This logic is voiced in an exemplary manner by Hegel in his interpretation of faith and the Enlightenment.

Thus far we have primarily been discussing theology (in the sense of a conception of God). Faith is understood as a reaction to a world experienced as essenceless, as a flight toward a distant God who becomes more and more an empty, and undetermined transcendent .

The essencelessness characterizing humankind and world in this context is brought to the fore all the more explicitly in what

24

Hegel holds is the dominant conception of actuality in the Enlightenment—namely, *utility*. A further elucidation of this clearly reveals the solidarity of theology, ontology, and anthropology in the logic of the absence of the essential. We have seen that religious faith does not stand its ground against the advance of critical reason. The latter thinks it can unmask the former as anthropomorphism. In this way the content of the essential is, in fact, brought back to earth. Formulated in another conceptual framework: the "projection" of faith is brought back or retracted. Faith itself becomes more and more abstract under the pressure of the critique. The essential (God) becomes less and less actual. By virtue of this movement, faith approaches the deism and agnosticism of the Enlightenment.

This forced separation between the absolute essence and finite actuality is not without repercussions on "this-side," on this finite actuality itself. If the absolute is *elsewhere* as an undetermined and unrecognizable highest being (as an abstraction that is hypostasized as a being), then what is not absolute is also transformed. It loses its depth. It is "purified" of all symbolic references (wood *is* now wood, bread *is* bread, nothing more, they are no longer symbols of the divine). All that exists is reduced to its *immediacy*: a finite sensible reality. Materialism—a position that sets the tone in the Enlightenment—is an important expression of this.

The reduction of everything to what can be experienced by the senses does not, however, mean that finite actuality acquires a new substantial quality. On the contrary, finite actuality loses all weight over against the pure insight of reason that absolutizes itself. It undergoes the same fate as the object of faith: the loss of all density. This is clear from the reigning ideology that results from the struggle of the Enlightenment—namely, *utilitarianism*.

The leading ontological and anthropological category is *utility* (*Nützlichkeit*). Hegel understands utility as an unsuccessful unity of two moments that logically characterize each being, in its universality—namely, its being in-itself and its being-for-another. This typically speculative-logical theory cannot be extensively dealt with here. I limit myself to a more global elucidation.

That which is useful is on the one hand *in-itself*: it would not be able to interest anyone if it did not have any intrinsic value. Yet, this being-in-itself cannot be called substantial: utility is as much *for-another*. For utility means that something only has a value in relation to something else. This means that the being-in-itself, the substantial quality of things, is reduced to a mere transitory moment, to something that dissolves once exposed to a self-consciousness that considers itself absolute. In the relation of utility, things are conceived of as independent, which are then negated as such, and thus not truly independent. Neither are they merely the embodiment of one's own subjectivity. The ontology of utilitarianism correlates with the anthropology of the pure insight that considers itself absolute. In the French Revolution this absolute freedom will appear, as Hegel further shows. This freedom will attempt to realize the entire ethical actuality from within itself: the absolute will no longer be "elsewhere," it will be here and now. I will not further elaborate on this problematic as it lies beyond the scope of the work. I limit myself to the category of utility in its immediate sense and will not go further into the "positive" sense it acquires in the further account of Hegel. Utility is the preeminent embodiment of the *absence of the essential*. Beings lose their weight when their meaning is reduced to their utility: their worth no longer lies in what they are in-themselves, but in what they are for an other.

The world of utility is one of complete relativity of each over against every other. Being-in-itself and being-for-an-other turn over into each other continuously. In the sphere of ethical relations this means, for example, that social ties are no longer rooted in the intrinsic worth of the participants (in their "nature"), but in reciprocal utility. Life in a community is no longer a good in itself, but merely a means toward the satisfaction of individual interests. This is clearly illustrated in most of the contract-theories by which social and political life are legitimated in the Enlightenment.[21]

Does utility not, however, imply an absolute Being—namely, the particular individual as the ultimate point of reference? Must this not be called the essence that is present? This is doubtful. It is rather that the loss of substantiality that characterizes the world of utility also affects one's own subjectivity. Moreover, the self is also reduced to its significance, or to what it can win for itself, within the utilitarian network. It becomes a function both in relation to others and in relation to itself; a function in a continually changing process of satisfying particular needs. Here the anthropology of *Le Neveu de Rameau* returns in another form, where the self is little more than a set of roles: *Tout le reste prend des positions*,"[22] every individual is an ephemeral link in the network of relations; nobody defines themselves from within themselves, but only in relation to others.

As is well known, Kant's ethics contains a fundamental critique of this dominance of utility. The leading principle of this critique is founded on the unconditional value of the human person: that we treat humanity in oneself and in others always also as an end in itself and never only as a means. In this we recognize *as in a contrast*, the anthropology typical of the logic of absence.

Whether one can justifiably call this logic the dominant understanding of being in our (post)modern culture, as is here proposed, no doubt will remain open to question. Who is in a position to understand adequately one's own time? The question is whether we can even properly speak of "our" time. Does this not primarily resemble a rather heterogeneous collection of different "times," different styles, language-games, and conceptions?[23] Nevertheless, this much is certain: to the extent that the logic of absence dominates the ruling understanding of being, usually implicitly, under the surface, as unquestionably self-evident, it blocks a free attitude to experiences of thought that come to an affirmation of God.

The chapter I now conclude will have achieved my aim if it contributes to the creation of a space in which these experiences speak anew. The following chapter ventures a modest "phenomenology" of "philosophical experiences" of the absolute.[24] Only when one is thoroughly conscious of what determines thought in its overriding direction can these experiences reveal themselves for what they are. As I said earlier, only subsequent to the phenomenology will the critique be developed. Among other things the question will be whether these experiences can sustain themselves. But first it is necessary to let them speak for themselves.

2
Ways of Thinking toward God

2.1 Faith and Thought

Faith—The God of the philosophers is not the God of Pascal.[1] This expression is not meant to sanction a prevailing opposition. The opposition is not at all a "fact" but the result of a particular *philosophical* interpretation. This interpretation remains, to a large extent, imprisoned in the logic of the understanding (*Verstand*) of the Enlightenment to which it is opposed. This logic has been sufficiently dealt with in the previous chapter. One of its characteristics is the opposition between faith and insight. With the above expression I want to highlight something else—namely, a difference in *experiential context* and *interest*.

A phenomenology and a philosophy of religious experience can show that we come to express the name of God on the basis of different fundamental experiences of actuality. Experiences of sense and nonsense, emotion and anxiety, being overcome and emptiness, guilt and goodness, suffering, beauty, thankfulness, unfathomable pain and incomprehensible anger. Such experiences are expressed in many different ways in a multiplicity of religious texts, symbolic stories, metaphors, myths, mystical "accounts," prayers, psalms, moral commandments, and so forth. These texts in turn influence the way those who are confronted by them experience life.

Experiences generating stories and stories guiding experiences: each of these is bound to ritual contexts. These offer forms of devotion and liturgy in which the content of these texts is "made manifest," re-iterated, confirmed, and personally appropriated. This is the place of the God of religion, the God who is invoked and worshipped, or with whom one dwells in meditation. He bears many names: JHWH, Father, the Holy, Future, Savior, Wisdom, Creator, Rock, Father of

29

Jesus, Justice, Power, and so forth.[2] This God is not an abstract entity, but is believed in as a living person, as absolute transcendence and at the same time as "more intimate to me than I am to myself."

This God does not appear as an answer to an intellectual problem (though we must not stop thinking if we believe). This God has an existential and practical significance. This God functions within the context of a horizon of meaning, of a view of life, of a worldview.[3] Its "truth" is not dependent upon syllogisms or sophisticated reasoning and has even less to do with the universality of the *sciences*. The truth of belief in God is existential and personal: its validity lies in the meaning it serves to provide within the context of a personal life. Neither acceptance by others, nor universal recognition of the believer's truth claims, are conditions for personal acceptance. This does not mean that faith is not also social. One's singular conviction is mediated and nourished by a community of fellow believers. Faith is not merely something interior, though it is, nonetheless, completely personal.

The God of Abraham, Isaac, and Jacob, the God of the Christian tradition, is rooted in an experiential context and is inseparable from a concern that is not philosophical. Of course, the question remains concerning the relation of this God to the God of the philosophers. This question can be motivated by faith itself. In that case the believer attempts to sound the rational content of his religious conviction: *fides quaerens intellectum*—faith seeking understanding.[4] The question can also concern the philosopher seeking to penetrate deeper into the bond between the results of one's own thoughtfulness and what springs from other sources.

Some will say that a philosophical concept of God is no more than a rational recuperation of views and images stemming from religious traditions. In that sense, there is no "God of the philosophers." Better formulated: such a God is no more than a pale, somewhat abstract shadow of what is present in full richness in religion. Of course, it is evident that the philosopher does not invent actuality. Hegel's dictum about philosophy being "its own time comprehended in thought (*ihre Zeit in Gedanken erfasst*)" expresses the point well. The question is: What does that mean?

The Experience of Thought—Philosophy is reflection, trying to bring to understanding what experience in the most encompassing sense brings about: actuality itself in its full concreteness. This "bringing to understanding" is not a mere repetition of all the world has to offer. It is more than the representation in language of what is. There is not only the content, the object of philosophy: full concreteness. But in addition to content, there is also the philosophical form, the specific manner of questioning and thinking that typifies philosophy. This form takes on different forms throughout the history of philosophy.

Philosophy is "a beloved with many faces."[5] Nevertheless, its constant concern is to understand, to explain, to see connections, to grasp the essence of something. Essential to this is the principle of the *autonomy* of thought. Philosophy is always a form of thinking for oneself, of critical and self-responsible insight, in one or another way always beginning anew on solid foundations.[6]

Because of its peculiar form, philosophy is more than the experience of existence which it tries to understand. Although entirely dependent on the culture in which it appears and the experiences there encountered, philosophy has its own form. Philosophy is not swallowed up by what it thinks. It is also an enterprise unto itself. It leads to new experiences. In other words, a person who philosophizes undergoes experiences in this particular sense: *experiences of thought.*

One takes distance from what is immediately given and becomes conscious of the particularity of each experience. One formulates technical concepts. One asks about the actuality and truth of the many different experiences. Proceeding from its own experience of thinking, philosophy here stands over against the experience of existence in its immediacy. Completely dependent on what exists, philosophy thus becomes the source of new experiences.[7] Is this not an ambiguous way of speaking which obscures the issue: to call the thoughtful assimilation of existential experience itself experience, thought's own proper experience? Not necessarily; and least of all if one specifies the respect in which the experience is taken. Such diverse respects are implied in the common-sense understanding of experience. Experiences can function as elements in a process of induction; they can be the building blocks, so to say, leading to more general concepts and ideas. They can also serve another function. They can break through given frameworks and call what is granted into question. In this respect we sometimes speak of "gaining experiences, in the sense of something new breaking through." And so we sometimes say: "that was quite an experience." What is at issue here is a unique process.

On the one hand, this process is negative: the experience consists in the surrender of a particular conception because it is controverted by what is presented to consciousness. On the other hand, it is a productive process because a new, more genuine content has come into being, a truer understanding of actuality and ourselves. Then "experience" points to a particular development undergone by thought. In this development, we must adjust or relinquish more and more conceptions of the world and ourselves, because it seems that things are different than we meant. If someone forces us to say what we mean, it seems we voice another actuality than the one we had in mind. Thinking is, as it were, constantly challenging itself to realize what is actually thought, thus testing whether what is thought can hold its ground. This movement of thought is motivated by what cannot become directly present. It is the realization of the desire for truth.

Great philosophical texts, texts we frequently reread, texts that have their own actuality, such texts offer us an account of such experiences of thought. Such texts also speak about God or about the Absolute. Usually their theme, with respect to content, is supplied by religious traditions or different worldviews. However, what they do with their theme, the way it is discussed, questioned, developed, situated, its systematic role in the totality of thought, points to something else, something specific.

In *Die onto-theologische Verfassung der Metaphysik* Heidegger poses the question: "How does God enter philosophy?" I will return later to the specific problematic which Heidegger develops in response to this question.[8] Generally, and in light of the previous observations, the question can be answered as follows: God enters philosophy on the grounds of specific experiences of thought. The "God of the philosophers" is the result of genuinely original questioning and thinking. God is given different names in the tradition: the Absolute, absolute perfection, first cause, necessary being, origin and telos, highest being or actuality, the true substance, the highest good, absolute spirit, and so forth. These names refer to specific philosophical experiences.

In the rest of this chapter, I will present and develop several *fundamental experiences of thought* which lead to an affirmation of God.

Philosophical considerations about God are often determined by religious convictions already present in the milieu in which one philosophizes. In the past they sometimes functioned as apologetic support for the religious affirmation of God. Nevertheless, they imply their own proper experiences of thought which constitute an autonomous philosophical moment. This is now our concern. We will not further develop the issue as to what light this sheds on the "God of Pascal." We limit ourselves to the formulation of the principle: the discourse concerning the God of philosophy formulates what, in any case, the God of faith must be, if God is to be taken as a genuine *actuality*.[9]

In what follows, two sorts of experiences of thought will be elaborated. They are privileged experiences that play a leading role in Western philosophy. One could call them two *faits primitifs* which reveal ways to God. The image of a *way* does not only refer to the traditional "proofs."[10] It is primarily suited for emphasizing God's *immanence,* by contrast to the logic of absence, and without regressing to naive, spontaneously fantastical representations of God's presence. *Way* points us well toward the dialectic of presence and absence which, I suggest, is the most important moment of every philosophical discourse about God.

2.2 ENIGMATIC CONTINGENCY

Why something at All . . . ?—The first type of experience of thought rises from everyday experience. It consists in explicitly bringing to the fore something given in our spontaneous knowledge of things. These things appear in a new light: they do not become other than they are, but now appear as they are. Only now is it evident how it stands with them. The philosophical experience has a truth function: it lets be seen what is, it lets things appear as they are. In this respect it is hermeneutical, an account of what immediately appears; it interprets what is the case. Which experience is, in fact, at issue here?

To undergo such an experience, the flow of a spontaneous contact with things must be broken. One must become, in keeping with Husserl, an observer who is not engaged. One must suspend existential involvement in the world and take time, the time of *attention* in which one dwells on what is, so that it can show itself as it is.

Should one succeed in this, the initial effect is commonly an experience of alienation. When the straightforward relation with things is broken by a kind of existential interruption, things themselves lose their immediate familiarity. It appears strange that one exists so easily and without disquiet. Persons, things, everything pertaining to one's familiar world, be they close or far away, lose their accustomed *weight*. Their existence now becomes something precarious. In coming, as it were, to be arrested reflexively, one feels the full power of *time*, a power always at work but not always noted. The *things* that envelop the self, filling existence, are but for a short time. They come into being and pass away. The *relations* which more or less weave the self into society turn out to be fragile, ephemeral, transient: there seems little to guarantee their permanence. Other persons who intimately belong to the lifeworld, whose absence one can hardly conceive (after all they constitute in part what one is) disappear beyond the horizon or die. At the same time others unexpectedly enter existence, new things and tasks fill life, other connections and contexts arise. Previously the "natural attitude" experienced the seemingly evident world as completely massive, as something that simply *is*; now this world becomes *light*.[11] It loses its density. It is, but it is now clear that once it was not and once again it will cease to be. In the inner depth of its being, it seems touched by something *negative*. It is not its own sovereign.

Such experiences can befall us in various ways. They can also be consciously provoked by ways of exercising attention and reflection. They bring with them their peculiar *mood*: alienation, uprootedness, anxiety, limitless wonder. They are most intense when the experience of *weightlessness* comes closest to our own being.

It is not easy to be open to the idea that once we were nothing and that again we will be nothing. Nor is it easy to let the idea communicate all its implications. It brings a certain disorientation. We know that *nothingness* is lodged in us, although we can barely represent the fact that we will again come not to be. We cannot be compared with any indifferent object which ceases to exist. To be self is to be a world of feelings, desires, insights, duties, relations, persons. For the self no more to be is the vanishing of this lived world into nothingness.

Being surrounds the self on all sides and is seemingly endless, hence it is difficult to conceive of it as affected by nothingness. This is usually veiled by an appearance of absoluteness being given to what just happens to be. Does anything exist as its own origin? Does anything at all hold itself in its own hands? Is there anything that can withdraw from the power of time? Is there no complete being? Are all beings marked by a flaw, a lack, an emptiness, a "nothingness"? Does anything at all succeed in definitely persisting in being (Spinoza)? And if one understands all beings from the perspective of the whole of which they are a part, does this not lead to further insight? Possibly, but in any case not to an Archimedean point where all would attain peace and permanency. No matter how far one investigates the strong interrelation of things and events in history or nature, no matter how daring our speculations about the universe, no matter how far we traverse endless time and space, we will never encounter such a point. Nothing seems to rest upon itself. Nothing is free of the cycle of coming to be and ceasing. Nowhere seems manifest a fullness of being containing the ground of its own being wholly within itself, a fullness that has always already surmounted every negativity and lack. Everything seems marked by such contingency and groundlessness that being itself becomes perplexing: "Why is there something and not rather nothing?"[12]

Perhaps this question sounds somewhat esoteric. This is by no means the case with the experiences from which it can arise. These experiences belong to the *Lebenswelt*. They are accessible to everyone. They are not the result of complicated philosophical arguments.

Nevertheless, they have stimulated and provoked philosophical thought in many ways.

One of the experiences of thought to which they have led has become a privileged context of philosophical discussion about God: the so-called *proof from contingency,* an important variant on what tradition has come to refer to as the *cosmological proof.* As will become clear, especially in the last chapter, the term "proof" is not felicitous. "Proof" now points more to scientific practice than to philosophical reflection. "Proof" is full of ambiguity. All the more reason then to be vigilant to the *matter itself.* We understand this "proof" as attempting to clarify and cope intelligibly with the experience of contingency. This is not an attempt *to solve the enigma of contingency, but to think it through to its furthest consequences.*

An Informational Intermezzo: Concerning Proofs of God—As is well known, the tradition distinguishes three classic types of proofs: the *ontological,* the *cosmological,* and the *teleological* (which includes but is not limited to the physico-theological proof). In addition, we sometimes speak of a *moral proof.* This focuses on moral experience which, when carried through to its end, leads to an affirmation of God. In a certain sense Kant, the great "opponent" of the classical proofs, represents such an approach. I say "in a certain sense" because "proving something" here assumes a very specific form. We are concerned with a *postulate* that starts from moral experience, in particular the incongruity between ethical duty and happiness. I will develop this "experience of thought" in the third section of the following chapter, after I have discussed Kant's critique.

The *ontological* proof is clearly the most decisive. As we will see, Kant reduces the validity of the two other proofs to the ontological proof. According to the ontological proof, the affirmation of God follows from a consideration of the concept of God as such. The "way" leads from the concept of the Absolute to its *existence.* This will be dealt with in the next section. The experience of thought here made more explicit has to do with the fundamental unity of thought and being. It was first formulated in its classic form by Anselm of Canterbury and was later reformulated and elaborated, particularly by Descartes and Hegel.

In a certain regard the *cosmological* proof develops in another direction: from finite *existence* to infinite being. Here the affirmation of God results from reflection on the peculiar nature of the world and worldly beings. The classic expression of this proof is found in Thomas Aquinas. In his *five ways* Thomas takes the following as his points of departure: the phenomenon of *movement* (God as the prime mover), *efficient causality* (God as the first cause), *contingency* (God as necessary being), the *degrees of being* (God as the most perfect being in whom all beings take part), and *final causality* (God as the highest intelligence who orders the totality of beings).

The *physico-theological* proof is a modern form of this last way. The teleological structure of the world leads to the affirmation of a divine intelligence.

Of the many variants of the cosmological proof, the proof from contingency has the most extensive "effective history" (*Wirkungsgeschichte*). In my exposition I take up the problem of contingency in the full sense. I do not limit it to the cosmos *stricto sensu*, but take into account the total experience of being: both the world and subjective existence.

As mentioned earlier, the way to God from contingency is not a maneuver to solve the enigma of contingency. It is more an attempt to follow contingency through to its ultimate consequences. The proof—as with all "proofs"—stands or falls with what can be indicated as the final basic presupposition—namely, *faith in reason* and in the possibility of a reasonable ground to existence. I will return to this point later.

An Example: Thomas Aquinas—Many models are available for a reconstruction of the "way" that is developed in philosophy from the enigma of contingency.[13] I begin our reconstruction with a short presentation of Thomas Aquinas's now classic form of the proof. The text of the *third way* contains all of the elements that play a role in the history of the proof in a simple, clear, and succinct manner.

After this presentation and a brief explanation I attempt a more systematic clarification of how and why contingency *can* lead to the affirmation of something absolute.[14] What follows, then, is not an exegesis of Aquinas. Thomas's text functions more as a classic illustration of a problematic which we, inspired by a variety of historical material, will try to think through in our own way:

> The third way is based on what need not be and on what must be, and runs as follows. Some of the things we come across can be but need not be, for we find them springing up and dying away, thus sometimes in being and sometimes not. Now everything cannot be like this, for a thing that need not be, once was not; and if everything need not be, once upon a time there was nothing. But if that were true, there would be nothing even now, because something that does not exist can only be brought into being by something already existing. So that if nothing was in being, nothing could be brought into being, and nothing would be in being now, which contradicts observation. Not everything therefore is the sort of thing that need not be; there has got to be something that must be. Now a thing that must be, may or may not owe this necessity to something else. But just as we must stop somewhere in a series of causes, so also in the series of things which must be and owe this to other things. One is forced therefore to suppose something which must be, and owes this to no other thing than itself; indeed it itself is the cause that other things must be. And all call this God.[15]

Though the point is not a detailed analysis and interpretation of the text, some explanation is needed to let this concrete illustration speak.

The possible (*possibile*)—translated by the term contingent—is conceived as that which can both be and not be, as is made clear by the fact that it comes to be and ceases to be.[16] It is opposed to the necessary: that which cannot not be, that which is not subject to the cycle of becoming and ceasing to be. The core of the proof is the thought that if there were only contingent things (these are: things that once came into being and which will once again cease to be, hence put between nothing and nothing), then simply nothing would exist. Contingent things can only exist—and this existence is beyond doubt—if they are grounded in a necessary being—namely, in a necessary being which is itself not caused. Moreover, the argument presupposes the validity of the principle of ontological causality. In addition, it assumes the impossibility of carrying the chain of caused necessary beings through to infinity.

We must put an end to this "infinite regression." This is achieved by affirming a being that is necessary and that does not in turn borrow its necessity from something else: a being uncaused, unconditional, and in that sense absolute. Note that the proof does not result in the affirmation of a spiritual reality that has to be conceived as a person, but in a necessary being that is not caused by anything else. The reference to religion at the end ("all call this God") is at the very least not fully covered by the argument. Furthermore, the proof presupposes—if it is to have the power to convince—the entire metaphysical world of Thomas.[17]

A Necessary Ground for All that is—The significance of the experience of thought voiced in Thomas's text, however, is not wholly bound to the concrete metaphysical worldview that serves as its context. After all, it concerns an experience of thought that is nearly universal in philosophy. Thus we can read Thomas's text and to a certain extent comprehend it. Like him we are intrigued by the same matter which drives us to think, even though this thought will perhaps use different categories to express what it has experienced.

Granting all differences, the matter uniting us with Thomas lies in *the wonder about the fact that beings are, while we continuously and in many ways recognize their fragility, their nothingness, and their lack of self-sufficiency.*[18] It lies in the enigma that beings *are*, even while they also are intimately affected by *not-being*. This is expressed in a completely different conceptual framework in Leibniz's question: *Pourqoui il y a plutot quelque chose que rien?* (Why is there something rather than nothing?).[19] It is differently conceived yet again in Heidegger's reformulation: *Warum ist überhaupt Seiendes und nicht vielmehr Nichts?* (Why is there anything at all, rather than nothing?).[20] Contingency challenges thought to account for it: *rationem rederre*. Why is contingency a challenge for thought that wants to comprehend? Why is it a privileged place from which a movement begins, perhaps leading to the affirmation of something

Absolute, of God? To understand this, we must go more deeply into the concept of contingency.

The point of departure is an elementary assessment: beings come and go, they come into being and cease to be. Though they *are*, they bear not-being within them. This not-being is just as actual as being. It is not just a speculative possibility. Being and not-being qualify beings in an equiprimordial manner. That is what we mean when we call them contingent. That something is contingent entails both that it *is*, and that it can also *not* be. Contingent is to be distinguished from *possible*, which means that something though not yet in being, still *can* be, because it is not contradictory. The contingent is not what it is in a neccessary manner. Its being appears to be a sort of *suspension* of the hegemony of nothingness. Every moment of its existence it hangs, as it were, above the abyss of nothingness.[21]

With this the being of beings becomes enigmatic. How can we understand that things are, while they are encompassed by nothingness? Could it not be equally possible that there would be nothing? But then do we know what we are saying? Would this be a case of assuming that beings *are*, in order to destroy them in a second moment? But it is unquestionable that beings are. How, then, and on what grounds, have they come to be and persist in being? Not by themselves, because as contingent they were once nothing. They must have come into being through something other, which for the above reason is to be called *necessary*.

Contingent means that something does not have in itself the ground or reason of its being. It has it in necessary being. But, if that necessary being in turn has its reason in an other, then the search for a ground remains open, and contingent being remains uncomprehended. That is why the level of immanent causality must be abandoned. What must take place is a *qualitative shift* to a transcendent, metaphysical causality. The absolute must be considered outside the possibly infinite series of beings necessitating each other. The question of the how and why of this or that being thus becomes a question of the ground, the *whence* of being as such. This shift is justified, because the addition of contingent beings to the series of contingent beings does not make the whole necessary!

If we want to account for the existence of this being, then we are ultimately concerned with the totality of beings. We must alter our direction and ask about something that is not itself a being among beings but of another order.

In the classic example of the way from contingency—namely, Thomas's text—this change in direction is not thematized. There are, however, sufficient alternative texts which reveal the necessity of this turn.[22] For Aquinas God is not a being among beings. God *is* their mysterious ground.[23] However, we are not concerned here with a commentary on Thomas. What matters is the philosophical way by which we are attempting to *comprehend*, to *ground*, and to account for being in its *enigmatic contingency*. It is essential here to highlight the qualitative turn. It marks the difference in this approach from the sciences. These operate with a concept of immanent causality. The question as to the *why* of a *particular being* does not lead the sciences to question the whence of *being as such*. The wonder that gives rise to scientific research and the motives that guide it (for example, being able to predict, control, and so forth) are of a different nature. Hence there is, for example, a radical qualitative distance between the hypothetical scientific "Big Bang," and the Absolute as ground of all that is.

The Decisive Presupposition—Until now we have proceeded as if it were unquestionably justified that thought, solicited by the radical contingency of being, completes the movement toward something absolute. But is that so? Must not the possibility of this transcending movement be itself grounded? Does not thought here lose its anchor in the safe base of "experience"?

As is well known, Kant has especially problematized this possibility. The following chapter will examine this fully. The experience of thought now under discussion will then be confronted with other experiences of thought which profoundly problematize the first one.

However, at this stage the point is not so much the general epistemological question of the possibilities and the limits of our cognitive faculty, but rather the contents which arise in the attempt at understanding contingency. The question of the justifiability of the transcending movement now concerns the *content* of this development of thought, not its formal possibility. In other words: Could it not be just as consistent and reasonable, given the nature of the very issue we are trying to think, *not* to complete this movement? Must contingent actuality have a ground or source of its being, "something" which constitutes and maintains its existence? Could one not just as well argue that contingent beings are *groundless*? A consideration of the essential bond between contingency and *time* can reveal the difficulty of this position, the difficulty of conceiving the contingent as *absolutely* groundless.[24]

The contingent is defined as that which comes into being and ceases to be, existing at a certain moment and not at another. Being contingent is being in time. If the contingent were not caused by something else, but completely groundless, then it would groundlessly enter time and groundlessly disappear. So it is not developed out of something else and is therefore withdrawn from the process of becoming. If so, it cannot be in time: neither can it begin nor end. Being in time means having a certain duration. Nothing can be purely punctual in time.

If the contingent were completely groundless, it would cease to be in its becoming, and become in its passing away: withdrawn from time, it would not endure. What is in time begins and ends, and so has a certain duration. Groundlessness would entail timelessness. Given this result, it would appear that thinking must correct itself. After all, it comes into direct conflict with itself, since at the beginning of our reflection contingency was defined as that which was marked by temporality.

The relationship with time reveals that the contingent cannot be thought as completely groundless. It is to be understood as that which is not its own ground, but as being grounded in something other.

Everything said here stands or falls with one great presupposition, historically given an exemplary formulation in Leibniz's principle of *sufficient reason*. Every way of thought toward God presupposes that there is a logic in things, that "reason governs the world" (Hegel), that "being is intelligible" (Thomas). This presupposition can of course be contested. It is, however, not possible to "found" this denial. To want to justify it implies practicing the principle being contested. With the denial of this presupposition, the entire problematic of this book falls (in no way does this mean that this presupposition is sufficient reason for the way of thought to God; it is merely a necessary condition). The "God of the philosophers" is after all "merely" a problem for philosophy, for a *thinking* which wants to understand all that is.

If every philosophical position one takes is reduced to a pure construction, or to a rhetorical turn in pursuit of power, not only does the possibility of a philosophical way to God vanish; it is also the end of philosophy and its dissolution into art or politics.

What is the overall result of this first experience of thought? Perhaps the most important result is that "something" forces itself to the fore—namely, that thought, in its attempt to comprehend the contingency of existence, confronts the idea of a highest reality which is both *necessary* and the *ground* of everything. This ground is *transcendent*: it is not a being among beings. This ground is *immanent*, because it is ground, it conquers the power of nothingness.

How this absolute is to be further understood—if that is even possible—is presently not under discussion. I will take this up again later. For now this point suffices: thinking can undergo experiences that result in the consideration that the essential is not absent. It is completely different from anything else, the ground of all that is. Such an actuality—God—is a necessary actuality. It cannot not exist, it is not caused by anything else, it is in that sense *groundless*. It is something that exists per definition; it is inconceivable *(essence)* that it does *not exist*.

This is a remarkable result. The first experience of thought leads us to the second. Formulated in traditional terms: the cosmological proof refers to the ontological.[25] The attempt at understanding contingency leads thought to a new task: to think of something whose essence contains its existence.

In the following section I reconstruct the movement of this second fundamental experience of thought. I also try to develop it further in our own terms.

2.3 THE ACTUALITY OF THOUGHT

Intermezzo—Are the traditional ways to God really experiences of *thought?* Is not all talk of God a disguised form of theology which formulates and clarifies a religious faith? Is the primary concern not experiences of faith instead of experiences of thought? In this intermezzo I dwell on this question, for we find the first explicit formulation of the ontological proof in the famous *Proslogion* of the medieval thinker Anselm. In this the existence of God is affirmed on the basis of a certain definition of God's essence—namely, "that than which nothing greater can be thought." The proof is situated in the context of a religious elevation. It appears as believers' attempt to clarify for themselves and for others the rationality of their faith in God. Moreover, the famous definition of the essence of God, *aliquid quo nihil maius cogitari possit* (something than which nothing greater can be thought) is represented as something which belongs to the content of *faith*: *et quidem credimus te esse aliquid quo nihil maius cogitari possit* [indeed, we believe You to be something than which nothing greater can be thought].[26] Does what remained implicit in the cosmological way now not seem obvious—namely, that a certain conviction of faith is crucial for the so-called experience of thought?

It is evident that the ontological proof is formulated in a culture which is completely permeated by the Christian religion. We have already pointed out that philosophical reflection does not begin from zero. It is always an attempt at a *rational* consideration of what is in one way or another given to prereflexively. This endeavor is characteristic of the philosophical experience, regardless of the source of the content given to the preunderstanding. Regardless of the genealogy of "that than which a greater cannot be thought," regardless of the context in which it took shape, the question for philosophical thought remains its rational content.[27] That this content has its own significance is clear not only from Anselm's text. Subsequent history also illustrates this. Particularly since Descartes it has played a properly philosophical role in the construction of great metaphysical systems. Kant criticized it as a rational theory. Later Hegel took it up again on purely speculative grounds.

This philosophical content is the issue in the following discussion. I will proceed as I did in the previous section. Via a paradigmatic illustration I will try to clarify the logic of the specific experience of thought here in question. This will include a reconstruction of Descartes's and Anselm's ideas. More general consequences will also be explored for the philosophical concept of God and the logic of absence.

Anselm: Thought and Being—Compared to the prevailing idea of what thought is and how it relates to actuality, Anselm's view in the *Proslogion* must appear as strange and perhaps even bizarre. Most often we understand thought as subjective, something proper to human activity, radically different from actuality and all that exists. That something is thought is one thing; that the object thought exists is something else. Thought and being stand opposite each other as the subjective and the objective.

Anselm has a different conception, rooted in a specific experience of thought. Among ideas one is unique: a thought we cannot think without affirming the being of what is thought. The point is not the unity of thought and being realized in actions: here thought as conscious purpose leads to action and comes to realization in that. Anselm is not concerned with a kind of poetic, productive thought. The strong connection between thought and being is different: to an understanding of this thought belongs an affirmation of the existence of what is thus thought. To the essence (*what* something is) belongs existence (*that* something is). According to Anselm, this is uniquely the case with the thought of God.

Anselm's view is truly *contre-coeur*. It goes against the prevailing opposition of thought (subjective) and being (objective). It does so at a point where the connection between thought and existence appears to be most problematic—namely, the case of the highest idea to which speculative thought can elevate itself. We can *think* what we want and attribute various degrees of reality to those diverse thoughts. With one thought, however, we have absolutely no choice: thinking God necessarily entails the affirmation of God's existence.

In the *Proslogion* Anselm formulates it as follows:[28]

> Therefore, Lord, giver of understanding to faith, grant me to understand—to the degree you deem best—that you exist, as we believe, and that you are what we believe you to be. Indeed, *we believe you to be something than which nothing greater can be thought*.[29] (*aliquid quo nihil maius cogitari possit*). Is there, then, no such nature as you, for the fool has said in his heart that God does not exist? But surely when this very fool hears the words "something than which nothing greater can be thought," he understands what he hears. And what he understands is in his understanding, even if he does not understand [judge] it to exist. Indeed, for a thing to be in the understanding is different from understanding [judging] that this thing exists. For when an artist envisions what he is about to paint, he has it in his understanding, but he does not yet understand [judge] that there exists what he has not yet painted. But after he has painted it, he has it in his understanding and he understands [judges] that what he has painted exists. So even the fool is convinced that something than which nothing greater can be thought exists at least in his understanding; for when he hears of this being, he understands [what he hears], and whatever is understood is in the understanding. But surely that than which a greater cannot be thought cannot be only in the understanding. For if it were only in the understanding, it could be thought to exist also in reality—which is greater [than existing only in the understanding]. Therefore, if that than which a greater cannot be thought existed only in the understanding, then that than which a greater *cannot* be thought would be that than which a greater *can* be thought! But surely this conclusion is impossible. Hence, without a doubt, something than which a greater cannot be thought exists both in the understanding and in reality. . . . Assuredly, this being exists so truly [really] that it cannot even be thought not to exist.[30]

Within the context of a faith seeking understanding (*fides quaerens intellectum*) an authentic philosophical thought is realized.

Among other things, this is clear from the fact that Anselm does not appeal to religious experience for his "proof." He appeals only to the power of the intellect. His point of departure is the thought: "something than which nothing greater can be thought." Everyone can understand this thought, even the one (the "fool" in Anselm's eyes[31]) who does not believe in God.

As C. Steel rightly remarked in his commentary, this formula is less a positive definition of the essence of God than a negative description. The point is not simply "a highest being" or "the greatest." The point is a definition which excludes everything not in accord with the greatness of the object. The object is so defined that it remains transcendent to the definition: nothing can be thought greater than this being. It is more a *rule* for thought (whosoever wishes to think God must follow the rule that nothing greater than God can be thought) than a positive content of thought (what is then the content of this being greater than which nothing can be thought?). With this, thought reaches its own limits. It cannot think anything higher—the "God" of the philosophers. Though this God remains to a certain extent formal, still something essential is said about God, namely, that existence must necessarily be predicated of this being.[32] What "compels" thought to do this? Two things: the principle that existence is a perfection and the principle of noncontradiction. Whoever wants to be consistent in thinking "that greater than which nothing can be thought," is obliged to affirm its existence: such a thing "must" exist. In the development of his logic Anselm is by no means naive. He knows that it is not sufficient to think of the most perfect country (the "lost island"), more perfect than all others (*le meilleur des mondes possibles*) in order for it to also exist.[33] He knows full well that *esse in intellectu* in no way implies *esse in re*. He is no adherent of a kind of easy idealism. The exception is this one thought where the implication holds—and that is his experience of thought.

This position has been the object of heavy criticism. In the following chapter I examine these critiques further. Now, in this "brief phenomenology," I primarily want to represent, as adequately as possible, the sort of experience of thought of which Anselm's text is a paradigmatic expression.

The core of this experience is the following. When thought goes to its outermost limits and tries to think that above which it can think nothing else, it touches on an enigmatic unity of thought and being. Thought is transcendental openness to all actuality. It experiences itself as not just a subjective construction; it has an ontological value such that the existence of what is thought can no longer be denied. Anselm's proof expresses the ontological dimension of thought or the rationality of being. The essential is no longer understood as absent. It is not separated from thought which is itself understood as more than merely subjective. The essential is present, but not in the manner of a thing, or as merely present to hand. This presence appears there where thinking seeks to go to the outermost limit.

At the same time Anselm's experience illustrates that what becomes present, simultaneously withdraws. His proof is not an imaginary movement in which God is objectified into something present to hand. Nor is it a movement in which one simply projects the perfection of one's own thought. After all, the one whose existence is being confirmed remains "transcendent in relation to the description."[34]

Descartes: Subjectivity and Infinitude—In line with Anselm, Descartes takes up and develops further, albeit with many variations, the idea that thought encounters an absolute actuality in an ultimate reflexive movement. As pointed out by D. Henrich, Descartes offers the base of various modern versions of the ontological proof. I will not, however, limit myself to this resumption of Anselm's proof by Descartes as worked out in the *fifth meditation* and briefly indicated in the *Principia nr. 14*. I will also discuss Descartes's reflections in the *third meditation*. There Descartes explicates the specific form of causality which is connected with the idea of the infinite (too high to have been caused by us). There again thinking comes to experience that, when it reaches the limits of its possibilities, it cannot but affirm the existence of an absolute actuality. God is the necessary implication of the most extreme reflexive movement of thought into itself.

Descartes's thought manifests a decisive shift in the history of Western thinking. With Hegel one could say that in modernity the spirit turns inwards and takes its ownmost thought as the indisputable point of departure. In the reflective act the I obtains indubitable self-certainty. This is expressed in the famous "I think, therefore I am"—*cogito ergo sum*. This certainty becomes the Archimedean point of the entire philosophical discourse. According to some, such as Heidegger, Descartes's philosophy is the first true philosophy of the subject: its self-certain subjectivity becomes the reference point for all actuality.[35] This philosophy also contains a very definite understanding of being: being is understood as *representation*. Something *is* when, as represented, it can be traced back to the certainty of the I representing everything to itself.

We need not now decide if one should go as far as Heidegger. Nevertheless, a change is visible in Descartes's philosophy which will leave deep traces in modern philosophy. In the Aristotelian-Thomistic tradition of the Middle Ages, the unity of thought and being, of concept and actuality, was essential. Now thinking is dissociated from its immediate and evident connection to beings.[36] Rifts begin to appear in the classical unity of ontology. Thought will reinforce its independence and explicitly assert itself, against actuality, as the most true, as yielding most certainty. This self-certain thought becomes the normative access to being. Here Descartes reflects, in part, what the practice of modern natural science implies.

Naturally, something analogous could be said of the classical philosophy of Plato and Aristotle: only in the theory to which philosophy leads does actuality show itself as what it *is*. Nevertheless, something more occurs with Descartes. Genuine thought is not only the normative access, it is the most real being or true substance. What is traditionally called *ousia*, substance, is developed by Descartes from the experience of thought itself, from the *cogito*. Substantiality no longer refers primarily to the rational order of nature or to the intelligible order of being, but to the certainty of the *I think*. For Descartes the subject does not yet play the role it will have later in modern philosophy starting with Kant.[37] Still one can argue—granting the necessary nuances—that with Descartes *substantiality* is primarily conceived in terms of subjectivity. The motives behind this important turn cannot be further considered here.[38]

In addition to this global characterization, I must point out the following. With Descartes the dominance of thinking subjectivity is accompanied by the affirmation of something that fundamentally transcends this subjectivity: God, the infinite, the most perfect being, the necessary being. What the religious tradition calls God, is conceived by Descartes as an infinite, *perfect* being that exists *necessarily*.[39]

Descartes here moves on the *border* between ancient and medieval thought and modernity. On this border he develops a specific experience of thought which I will now try to clarify. Its core is this: insight into the substantiality of one's ownmost thought leads to an affirmation of God. Going to its limits, thinking touches on an absolute actuality. This does not act as a hypothesis or a postulate, but as a being that becomes present in thinking itself.

God as Ground and Measure—The metaphysical affirmation of God in Descartes's work is not a kind of addendum. It is not a foreign body at odds with the whole. It is more than a "medieval remnant." According to the logic of his "philosophical experiment," the affirmation of God is an essential implication of the certitude of one's thinking subjectivity.

In the *cogito*, Descartes looks for the indubitable foundation for any further knowledge and for the construction of a metaphysics which will unfold the truth of all that is. The " I think" is a point of indubitable certainty: "let whoever can do so deceive me, he will never bring it about that I am nothing, so long as I continue to think I am something."[40] Even if I were completely imprisoned in all sorts of illusions, even if the entire universe were controlled by diabolical and deceitful powers, even if all truth were mere appearance, the certainty of the *cogito* would not be affected. Here the thinking I is sufficient unto itself.

Now something remarkable occurs in Descartes. The power which brings down the entire universe in the experiment of methodological doubt is not able to rebuild the whole again from the *cogito*.[41] Through its own power the *cogito* cannot win back the actuality it bracketed in the experiment. A detour via God is necessary: God—an infinite perfect being that does not deceive, that does not (cannot?) make nonexistent what I regard as clear and distinct. Only once it is proven that, with regard to what is evident to the mind, one is not deceived by a malicious God, can Descartes carry out the metaphysical reconstruction he has in mind. The question of the systematic validity of this approach is not central to our subject matter. We must focus on what makes it *necessary* for thinking to affirm God.

At first sight, the appeal to God seems like an argument from external authority: the last guarantee for the truth and actuality of clear and distinct ideas. In fact, it is something *to which thinking knows itself to be compelled* when it explores itself according to its utmost possibilities. Descartes' *third meditation* offers us the *first* account of this exploration.[42] One can doubt everything. Yet one cannot doubt the thinking, doubting subjectivity itself. One cannot doubt the *cogito*. But what is that? In the *second meditation* Descartes writes: "A thinking thing that thinks. What is that? A thing that doubts, understands, affirms, denies, is willing, is unwilling, and also imagines and has sensory perceptions."[43] A subjectivity of representations, of that we are certain. But what is the status of these representations (ideas)? What are they? What is their nature? Where do they come from? They are all *my* ideas—hence they are *formally* equivalent. However, concerning their *content* the differences are great. The idea "red" is of a different type than the idea "substance" or "extension" or "movement" and so forth.[44] Might they not all be produced by me, constructions of thinking subjectivity? Descartes leaves this option open. Perhaps I might form the idea of other people from the idea of the *res cogitans* as a substance? The determining factor is that the degree of being of these ideas does not exceed that of my own I. Only what lies within my ability can be constructed by me because, as Descartes says: "it is manifest by the natural light that there must be at least as much . . . in the efficient and total cause as in the effect of that cause. For where, I ask, could the effect get its reality from, if not from the cause."[45]

In principle all representations should be reducible to the productive activity of the *cogito*. For neither natural things nor other people represent ideas which exceed the power of thinking subjectivity. Nevertheless, on this point, where the scope of the power of thought is measured, its limits also become apparent. After all, in its self-reflexive turn inwards, the subject stumbles on a representation which, though present within, resists its constructive activity. This is the representation *God*. According to Descartes, this is the representation of a "substance that is infinite, eternal, unchangeable, independent, supremely intelligent, [and] supremely powerful."[46]

This representation does not find its ground in the *cogito*. Why? because of the imperfection and finitude of the human being. My finitude emerges in every moment of my existence: I doubt, I make mistakes, I have all sorts of needs. The idea of God is too great for me to be able to produce it.

So I must have received it from a being whose power of being corresponds to the content of that idea. That I have an idea of God as an infinite and perfect being proves that God, as truly existing, placed the idea in me. *After all, on my own I cannot construct it.*

But is that really so? Could the idea of the infinite still result from my own thinking activity—namely, as the effect of the negation of all finitude? Descartes rejects this possibility, because the idea of infinitude is not just a negative idea. There is more to the idea of the infinite than the idea of a negated finitude. Descartes thinks that the relations should be reversed. One's own limitation and finitude do not produce the infinite, but are, to the contrary, only possible because of the idea of the infinite. I only recognize myself as finite by comparing myself with what I am not—namely an infinite being.

Of course, I cannot understand God in the fullness of divine being. God's actuality surpasses any conception which I, as a finite being, could form of God. Still the idea of the infinite is sufficiently clear and distinct to see that its positive reality transcends anything produced by the *cogito*.[47]

Many, including Mersenne and Hobbes, have argued against this position.[48] Is God's infinitude really more than the realization of one's own limitation? Is it not just the maximization of one's own perfections? In response Descartes stands by his fundamental insights. Where does the ability to maximize all finite perfections in a highest being come from? The answer is clear: because rather than creating it, we *encounter* the representation of God in ourselves. That is why we can, as it were, surpass what we are. In this sense the idea of the infinite precedes the idea of the finite: "my perception of the infinite, that is God, is in some way prior to my perception of the finite, that is myself. For how could I understand that I doubted or desired—that I lacked something—and that I was not wholly perfect, unless there were in me some idea of a more perfect being which enabled me to recognize my own defects by comparison?"[49] Descartes is resolute: God is not a construction based on one's own imperfection and longing for perfection. No, the realization of one's finitude is the effect of an always already present idea of the infinite.

Nevertheless, Mersenne's objection continues to make problematic the way of demonstration: "the idea of a perfect being [God] is nothing more than a conceptual entity, which has no more nobility than your mind which is thinking."[50]

Put otherwise: What guarantees that *existence* corresponds to this representation? For those unsatisfied with the answer given above, Descartes has had an other experience of thought. We find an account of this in the *fifth meditation*. Its essential logic is formulated in the *Principia, nr. 14*. What we see here is a variation of Anselm's proof. Yet it involves important new elements, which become most apparent if we include Descartes's answers to his contemporaries.

In the *fifth meditation* Descartes writes:

> But when I concentrate more carefully, it is quite evident that existence can no more be separated from the essence of God than the fact that its three angles equal two right angles can be separated from the idea of a triangle, or that the idea of a mountain can be separated from the essence of a valley. Hence it is just as much of a contradiction to think of God (that is, a supremely perfect being) lacking existence (that is, lacking perfection), as it is to think of a mountain without a valley.[51]

Descartes was quite conscious of the fact that such an argument was susceptible to misinterpretation. This appears also in the many objections of his contemporaries. Surely it is not enough to think something exists in order for it to be real? I can imagine a winged horse, but nothing exists in reality on that account! Surely my thought does not impose any necessity on things?[52] Does the argument say anything more than that the *idea* of a highest being is bound up with the *idea* of existence? We do not need to reconstruct the entire debate.[53] I limit myself to the essence of the discussion: this is, as it were, Descartes's only reply, presented by him in a variety of ways. In the case of God, the relationship between *essence* and *existence* is not arbitrary. In the same way that the triangle and the sum of its angles being 180 degrees cannot be conceived separately, so it is with God and existence. This is not a relationship which we have constructed ourselves, nor is it a question of purely nominal definition. Above all it is a *unique* case in which idea and existence are necessarily related. The clear and distinct idea of a body, for example, does not necessarily imply its existence. With God it is otherwise. We think of God as the most perfect being, the highest, *most powerful*, who lacks nothing and does not depend on anything else, as that which is completely through itself, without cause, existing completely on its own power and in that sense, necessary. Such a being implies existence.

It is especially the attribute of *power* (*summa potentia, immensa potestas*) which allows Descartes to parry the objections. One could object that the idea of perfection remains somewhat arbitrary. Who decides what belongs to it? It seems like the maximalization of the particular perfections which co-exist in nature. But this is not so with the idea of the highest power of being: in no way is it dependent on anything else for its existence. This must be thought as necessarily existing.[54] What is important in Descartes's consideration is the stress on "not being able to do otherwise." We can represent all sorts of things. We can construct winged horses, ideal societies, golden mountains. We are free to add or subtract from these what we wish. However, when we think God as the highest, most perfect, almighty being we are no longer free to add or subtract existence.

Descartes expresses the experience of dealing with what exceeds any subjective arbitrary choice. When thinking goes to its utmost limits, it finds itself constrained to affirm the existence of what it thinks. It has the experience that the essential is not absent, but that for thinking it is *present actuality*.

Essence and existence are different; more precisely, with the essence existence is not necessarily given—that is correct for finite beings. It does not hold for God. Here thought has to do with a logic over which it does not freely decide.

In his book *Der Gott der neuzeitlichen Metaphysik,* W. Schulz has given form to Descartes's experience of thought in the context of the *finitude* so dominant in modern philosophy. In this he resists Heidegger's interpretation of modern philosophy and particularly of Descartes's role. According to Heidegger, Descartes's philosophy represents an ontology from the standpoint of human subjectivity: *"insofern sie den Menschen als Bezugsmitte des Seienden aus seinem eigenen Selbstbewusstsein her sichert.*[55] Descartes's metaphysics would be a metaphysics of subjectivity in which subjectivity is the ultimate point of reference for all actuality. Against this, Schulz stresses that Descartes's metaphysics does not entail a simple bringing to the fore of the self-conscious I, but that God is posited above the I as the true subject which sustains and determines the world in its totality, including humankind.[56]

The proof of God is an illustration of this. It not only demonstrates that the idea of God cannot be produced by me, but also—and this is essential for Schulz's interpretation—that the awareness of myself as a *finite* being is only possible against the background of the idea of God. "The idea of God is posited simultaneously with the idea of the I . . . as a *counter concept over* against my own being. Therefore, I cannot guarantee this idea."[57] Grasping one's own subjectivity always implies understanding such a finite subjectivity in opposition to the infinite.

Schulz argues that in this respect Descartes's proof has another tenor than the proofs of the Middle Ages. It is a type of *e contrario* proof: *the attempt to manage completely without God fails, precisely because of its leading perspective—namely, that of insight into one's finitude.* The philosopher discovers that one cannot ground God on one's own finitude. God's infinitude and human finitude belong together, because only human beings who comprehend their finitude through the idea of God are compelled to place God above themselves as the other of self. God is only a meaningful actuality from the perspective of consent to one's finitude.[58] According to Schulz, for Descartes God is not just a concept, but the *measure* which is set above and against me by an inner necessity, in relation to which I recognize myself as finite.[59]

Descartes's approach contains the idea that the finite human being, in order to understand itself as finite, must presuppose God. This presupposition is not a hypothesis, it is to have knowledge of the presence of the Absolute.

2.4 THE EXPERIENCE OF LIMITS AND OPENNESS

From the above it appears that the affirmation of God lies in drawing out further the experience of the limits of one's ownmost thought.

Limits can only be experienced *as* limits when, in one way or another, we are also beyond them. The "thoughtful experience" of God is not reducible to the incomprehensible conclusion of an encounter with an utterly strange alterity. The absolute does not appear in thought as a wholly indeterminate and unknown X.

Rather it is that to which one is most intimately bound—usually in an implicit or nonthematic way. One does not "know" this immediately nor directly, but via an exploration of the human spirit and its furthest limits. In the experiences of thought constructed and reconstructed in this chapter, the human spirit has revealed itself as openness to the Absolute. This transcendental openness entails more than the fact that finitude, albeit radical, is not absolute. It is more than *empty openness* to what is indeterminate and entirely withdrawn into itself. In its full extent, this transcendental openness rather points to a communication with God which permeates every fiber of existence. The *experiences of thought* discussed not only open a perspective on *God*. They unveil something about the *human being:* how the human must be conceived for these experience of thought of the Absolute to be possible. It is comparable to the relation between ethics and ontology in Kant. Ethical experience, the consciousness of an unconditional "ought," compels us to certain postulates about the human. Moral duty is the ground of knowing of freedom: it necessitates us to think of the human being as a free and responsible being. So also awareness of the Absolute points to the transcendental openness of the human spirit. This openness is not to be understood as a sort of empty and open-ended anthropology. It is rather—and this might seem paradoxical—a *being filled with* the infinite and a participation in all that is, or an inexhaustible depth which makes the awareness of finitude possible.

The theme of limit and openness has become classic in Western philosophy. We hear it already in the famous words of Heraclitus: "One could never discover the limits of the soul, should one traverse every road—so deep a measure does it possess."[60] It comes to expression in Aristotle's "the soul is, in a certain way, everything" (*pychè pôs pantá*) and in Thomas's equivalent *Anima quodammodo omnia*.[61] It is present in Descartes's *l'ide de l'infini* and in Hegel's metaphysics of Spirit. It is present in Plato's theory of Eros[62] and in a very particular way in his doctrine on *anamnesis* or recollection.

According to Plato, the soul is able to have knowledge of the Ideas because it has beheld them in its previous existence, prior to the incarnation in the body. That is why knowledge of the Ideas occurs by way of recollection and recognition. This is in line with Socrates' maieutic conception of philosophy: the deepest truth need not be delivered from outside. We bear it within ourselves. True knowing is the explication of what is latent, present deeply within us.

Plato's doctrine of *anamnesis* has been the object of all sorts of criticism: to remember something of when one was not yet alive! Yet the doctrine can be more than an obscure thesis about what we knew before we existed as now we do. What Plato presents in quasimythological terminology can take on a deeper meaning, without becoming a profundity which merely spreads darkness. This is what J. L. Chrétien has recently suggested.[63] In this line one could interpret Plato's text on *anamnesis* as an expression of the *dialectic of finitude and openness* that marks existence. The soul's participation in the

Ideas reveals the transcendental openness belonging to the spirit. This openness is the condition of possibility of the experience which thought undergoes when it puts its utmost possibilities to the test and arrives at the limits of its capacities. Just as God is not a being but must be understood as the ground of beings, so this openness is not a determinable place, but a dimension which must be posited if one wants to account for what one thinks.

The doctrine of *anamnesis* expresses even more. In Plato's language the understanding of the Ideas stands for the event of truth. This understanding does not alienate the I from itself but, to the contrary, brings it to its true being and to the true being of the world. What is the most *intimate*—that one is at home in the truth—must be also thought as the *most strange*. The doctrine of *anamnesis* is an expression of this paradox, itself intimate to truth. What we are in our deepest self, *we have not constituted*. It is given to us. That we can understand the Ideas, in our terminology, that we are oriented toward truth, is not something we ourselves have made, though we are never more at home than in the truth. Our own identity surpasses us, in the sense that the Other is the source of our ownmost I. The Absolute does not lie outside ourselves as a strange reality, but is *"ours"* as the *"Other"* that constitutes our own being. This also implies that what is most essentially and personally "ours," is not a secure possession. We have received it. Here God is not the light that blinds us nor the power which pushes our being aside. The paradox, wherein identity and alterity are held together, far surpasses an anthropocentrism which understands all relations between God and humankind within the master-slave dialectic (this dialectic rejects God as a negation of selfhood and freedom, as we see with Sartre). God is the wholly other that also is the very source of our being. The strange and the intimate imply each other. Being determined and being free go together, as in the way they go together with love on the human level.

Here thought also reaches its limits. The dialectic of alterity and identity, of limit and transcendental openness, of finitude and infinitude, is not a formula just to solve a problem. It is more a task for thought.

In the following chapters I try to realize something of this task.

In different contexts the same issue comes to the fore: the experience of *finitude*. Consciousness also undergoes this experience when seeking to understand how it stands with itself and the world. How is this related to the experiences above clarified as leading to the affirmation of God? Do they hold good?

3

An Abyss for Thought

Are the experiences of thought developed in the last chapter immune to criticism? Of course, every philosophical position is always criticized in one way or another. But what are we to make of a critique that contests the entire undertaking?

For many, particularly after Kant's *Critique of Pure Reason*, the issue is clear: rational knowledge of God must be exposed as illusory. Thought allows itself to be led astray into positions which far exceed its proper powers. It is dragged along to a place where it does not belong. It tries ways which turn out to be *Holzwege*. In this context Kant says the following in the *Critique of Pure Reason*:

> Unconditioned necessity, which we so indispensably require as the last bearer of all things, is for human reason the veritable abyss. . . . We cannot put aside, and yet also cannot endure the thought, that a being, which we represent to ourselves as supreme amongst all possible beings, should, as it were, say to itself: 'I am from eternity to eternity, and outside me there is nothing save what is it through my will, *but whence then am I?*' All support here fails us; and the *greatest* perfection, no less than the *least* perfection, is unsubstantial and baseless for the merely speculative reason, which makes not the least effort to retain either the one or the other, and feels indeed no loss in allowing them to vanish entirely.[1]

Kant pleads for a limitation of our knowledge claims. The available material provides insufficient support to erect a speculative philosophical theory of God. Only with this self-imposed limitation does certainty arises in the domain of pure reason. Kant writes:

This domain is an island, enclosed by nature itself within unalterable limits. It is the land of truth (enchanting name!) surrounded by a wide and stormy ocean, the native home of illusion, where many a fog bank and many swiftly melting icebergs give the deceptive appearance of farther shores, deluding the adventurous seafarer ever anew with empty hopes, and engaging him in enterprises which he can never abandon and yet is unable to carry to completion.[2]

When it comes to philosophical ways to God are we dealing with such adventures? In the *Preface* to the first edition of the *Critique of Pure Reason* Kant speaks of questions posed by human reason "which, as prescribed by the very nature of reason itself, it is not able to ignore, but which, as transcending all its powers, it is also not able to answer."[3] As in the texts of Thomas, Anselm, Descartes, Hegel, and others, Kant's texts provide an account of experiences which thought undergoes when it tries to reach its utmost limits. The result, however, appears to be completely different. It is claimed that thought goes too far, that it lets itself be led astray by its proper speculative dynamic into statements whose meaning it cannot unambiguously establish. Kant's philosophy not only encourages us to think for ourselves, but more so encourages us to accept the limitations of reason's capacities.

The first chapter endeavored to clarify the logic that perhaps tacitly governs our thought and blocks philosophical ways toward God. This clarification opened the space for a reconstruction and an appropriate elaboration of a philosophical affirmation of God. But this positive illustration is insufficient. After the relatively unprejudiced way of the second chapter, I must now again assume some distance. If what was developed there is to endure, it must pass through the *purgatory* of criticism.[4] This critique is very extensive and varied. Yet, in its effective history (*Wirkungsgeschichte*) Kant's philosophy appears as a decisive and repeatedly reaffirmed position. Hence my choice in this chapter.

The first section contains a global presentation of Kant's critique. The next section clarifies those presuppositions crucial for the critique. Thus I try to gauge the extent of the critique. Finally, in the third section, Kant's critical turn is elaborated in a positive sense. Kant's philosophy is understood as a thinking that reveals, in an original fashion, the openness of our mind to God.

3.1 THE LIMITS OF THOUGHT

The Decisive Point: Thought and Being—"'Being' is obviously not a real predicate; that is, it is not a concept of something which could be added to the concept of a thing."[5]

This famous statement of Kant has served for many as a definitive refutation of the so-called ontological proof, of the the way used especially by Anselm and Descartes (and Hegel, but more on this later). According to Kant, the ontological proof is the most decisive. As will become apparent, it is implicated in all other types of proofs.

Considered globally Kant's critique develops along two lines.

The first line starts with the concept of an absolutely *necessary* being. In the ontological proof, God is thought of as the being to which existence belongs necessarily. God cannot possibly be conceived as nonexistent, and because of this God is necessary. This is precisely the difference with all other beings. They are contingent: they are but they could also not have been. They do not have what characterizes God—namely, a necessary link between the subject and the predicate *"existence."* The ontological proof draws its strength from the logical requirement of noncontradiction. With respect to God it would be contradictory to affirm the subject and deny the predicate. Nevertheless, on closer inspection this strength turns out to be but a weakness. According to Kant, some have tried to clarify the argument by referring to other similar judgments, such as, for example, the fact that to the concept of a triangle (the subject) necessarily belong three angles (predicate).[6] One cannot simultaneously posit a triangle and deny that it has three angles.

This clearly reveals the weakness of the ontological proof. The necessity in question only concerns the judgment, thus the *link* between subject and predicate. Thus the necessity is *conditional*: "The absolute necessity of the judgment is only a conditioned necessity of the thing, or of the predicate in the judgment."[7] Only under the condition that a triangle is *given* are the three angles necessary and is it contradictory to deny them. However, it is not contradictory to deny both subject and predicate or both the triangle and its three angles: "But if we reject subject and predicate alike, there is no contradiction; for nothing is then left that can be contradicted."[8]

What holds for geometrical judgments also applies to the judgment about God. It merely contains a conditional necessity. *If* I posit the concept of God as the absolutely perfect being, then I must affirm the existence of that being. In this case the negation of the predicate is contradictory, as is the affirmation of God while denying God's omnipotence. Due to this conditional necessity God's existence is not yet established. After all, it has not been established that we must posit God. I can deny both subject (God) and predicate (necessary existence) without contradiction. Here comes to light the essential point in Kant's argument against the ontological proof: the confusion of the *necessity of thought* with the *necessity of existence*. The proof fails because it makes an illegitimate transition from the order of thought to the order of existence.

This is obvious in the second line along which Kant's critique develops.[9] According to Kant, one might still try this way out. One might endorse the above critique, and yet maintain that there is one subject that is an exception to this critique: "namely, that there is one concept, and indeed only one, in reference to which the not-being or rejection of its object is in itself contradictory, namely, the concept of the *ens realissimum*."[10]

The point here is that only one subject must necessarily be affirmed because this very necessity is implied in the concept of absolute perfection. Here the focus is not on the link between subject and predicate, but on the subject itself. This subject cannot be denied without contradiction, because the most perfect being contains all of reality, all possible perfections, including the perfection of "existence."

Kant strenuously rejects this line of reasoning. His rejection is supported by the idea that *existence* is not a perfection: "Being is obviously not a real predicate; that is, it is not a concept of something which could be added to the concept of a thing."[11] Kant does not here argue that "being" is not a predicate. He says that it is not a *real* predicate. The term "real" is essential here. He refers to the table of categories in the *Critique of Pure Reason*, specifically to the first category of the second group which is entitled *quality*. This first category is entitled *Reality*.[12] Reality does not mean actuality in the sense of objective existence—this is what is meant when we say that "this is a real house, not just a possible house." Reality means what belongs intrinsically to the qualitative content of a thing. To the reality of a thing belongs everything which determines the *what*, the essence, of a thing, everything that is implied in the concept of something, all the properties of a thing.

Contrasted to this is *Sein* (Being) in the sense of *Dasein* (and not in the sense of a mere logical copula), a category of modality. It only serves to indicate that now an object actually corresponds to the qualitatively determined thing. Then *Being* points only to the "being posited" of something: something is no longer just possible, but it now actually exists. Hence Kant's famous example: the concept of a hundred actual talers does not contain any more than the concept of a hundred possible talers. If I have designated all the qualities of a thing and then I say in addition that it *is*, I do not add a new quality (for example besides God's wisdom, omnipotence, justice, and so forth). I only say that a determinate conceptual content also *exists*.

In the ontological proof, on the other hand, existence is considered as something *qualitative*. In Kant's reformulation of the ontological proof, God is presented as the *ens realissimum*, thus as the being which contains all possible (positive) predicates in itself.[13] Such a being must necessarily exist. Were it not to exist, it would miss a predicate, a perfection—namely existence. This would be a contradiction: affirming and simultaneously denying God as the most perfect being. In Kant's interpretation of "existence" such a contradiction is out of the question. What is compelling in the ontological proof seems to lapse.

What then is the relationship between subject (God) and predicate (existence)? In the ontological argument it is understood to be an *analytic* relation. The concept "God" contains "existence." But we know that is not allowed, because existence does not belong to the content of a concept. If we act as though this is the case, our success is very meager: the argument is then merely *tautological*.

To all appearances it seems that we conclude to existence from the concept; in fact, contrary to any logic, what is found as predicate is first smuggled into the concept. What is unjustifiably assumed in the subject and what precisely must be proven, is merely repeated in the predicate—namely, that the most perfect being also exists!

For the ontological argument *actually* to prove something, the judgment must be understood as *synthetic*. The affirmation of existence transcends qualitative determination. In this instance, the predicate existence can be denied without contradiction, because this is the case only in an analytical relation.[14]

Kant's whole argument is focused on the fundamental error of the ontological argument, namely, the confusion of a logical with a real predicate, of the order of thought and the order of being. We cannot conclude to existence from the logical possibility of a thing.

How then must existence be proven? Only by starting from what the ontological argument excludes—namely, experience.[15] Kant writes: "Whatever, therefore, and however much, our concept of an object may contain, we must go outside it, if we are to ascribe existence to the object."[16] Outside the concept means *in* the domain of *experience* determined by the senses: "Our consciousness of all existence . . . belongs exclusively to the unity of experience." The ontological proof can never succeed. In what Descartes attempted, "much labor and effort [is] lost. . . ."[17] It is like saying that a salesman can improve his or her actual financial situation by adding a few zeros to their cash account.

This does not mean that we have proved the impossibility of something existing outside the field of (sensible) experience. It only proves that the issue cannot be decided in purely theoretical terms.

Contingency—But does the so-called cosmological proof, Kant's term for the proof from contingency, not start out from the world of experience? Though this is the case, for Kant this way is also invalid. Within the cosmological proof "lies hidden a whole nest of dialectical presumptions."[18] Kant reconstructs the traditional proof as follows.

The point of departure is experience: the existence of something. Kant takes that in its minimal form: "Now I, at least, exist."[20] Traditionally existence is understood more broadly as all that is given in experience. Since, according to Kant, we call the possible object of all experience the *world*, we can speak of a cosmological proof. But the designation "proof from contingency" is more instructive. After all, the first step of the proof depends on contingency.

According to Kant, if *something* exists, then an absolutely necessary being must also exist.[21] In this first step of the proof, use is made of the category of causality. Everything that exists must have a cause. Indeed, empirically given beings are not the ground of their own existence. They are contingent and owe their existence to something else. However, if their cause is, in turn, itself accidental, it calls up yet another cause, which is in turn again caused, and so on. Contingent being is only sufficiently grounded when the endless causal chain comes to an end in a being that is no longer contingent but necessary. Itself caused by nothing else, it is the unconditional cause of all things. With this we have not yet arrived at the existence of God, the existence of an absolutely perfect being. The transition from a necessary being to an absolutely perfect being (an *ens realissimum*) constitutes the second phase of the proof. According to Kant, this occurs by showing that the necessary being must be defined as the most perfect being.

For the necessary being must be conceived as something that is *completely* determined (*durchgängig bestimmt*) through its own concept.[22] It must always be determined by one predicate out of all possible opposite predicates. In other words, it cannot contain anything indeterminate by which something might or might not befall it. If any potentiality or possibility remained, this being would be contingent and not necessary. It could still become this or that, and thus would not be completely determined. There is, for Kant, only one possible concept of a thing which a priori completely determines this thing—namely, the concept of the most perfect being, the *ens realissimum*: God as inclusive of, and origin of, all possible predicates. It follows that the absolutely necessary being can only be understood in terms of the absolutely perfect being—that is, God. So the second phase leads to the affirmation of God via the identification of the necessary being with the absolutely perfect being.

So far Kant's *reconstruction*. His *critique* of this is quite vehement. A first objection is that the cosmological proof makes use of a misleading maneuver (*eine List derselben*).[23] It appeals to experience. Thus it wants to guard itself against the critique of the ontological proof which viewed success as only possible by way of pure a priori concepts. In the end, however, this trick cannot succeed. When it really comes down to it, in this second phase, everything stands or falls with an argument we already encountered in the ontological proof. This second phase begins with the *concept* of an absolutely *necessary being*. To determine now the qualities of this concept, experience can no longer help us. Here reason takes leave of experience and loses itself in merely conceptual speculations. It turns out that the cosmological proof supposes the validity of the ontological proof. For what enables us to determine the necessary being as the absolute perfect being, what guarantees the *transition* from the one to the other? According to Kant, the ontological argument alone. On a purely logical level, necessity and perfection cannot simply be identified. It is not difficult to think of something that is necessary but nevertheless imperfect.

The identification is only given by the concept of the absolutely perfect being, which is precisely the core of the ontological proof. Identifying the necessary being with the perfect being is in fact deriving the necessary being from the concept of the perfect being. But this is exactly what happens in the ontological proof. There it is claimed that the perfect being exists necessarily. This identification, required for the success of the cosmological proof, is only possible because it is a priori contained in the concept of the most perfect being. People act as if a *transition* from necessity to perfection has taken place, while in fact this transition is only possible because "perfect" *implies* necessity. Hence, the cosmological proof can be traced back to the ontological proof. It is therefore invalid.

For Kant this invalidity is already visible in the first phase. He limits himself to a brief summary of the "dialectical tricks" (*Alle*

Blendwerk im Schliessen . . .).[24] Kant thinks that the experienced reader should be able to develop the rest.[25]

Everything comes down to an illegitimate use of the *principle of causality*. This principle guides the transition from the contingent to the necessary. Via this principle one *transcends* the world of (sense) experience, because the necessary being, which is the cause of everything, is not an object of any experience. It is something which people conclude on the basis of pure reason. For Kant this is completely illegitimate. The category "causality," just as all the other categories of the understanding, can only be utilized legitimately within the world of experience. "But in the cosmological proof it is precisely in order to enable us to advance beyond the sensible world [this is in principle impossible!] that it [the principle of causality] is employed."[26]

In addition, the argument assumes that an infinite series of causes is impossible. The series must terminate with a cause that, as first cause, exists unconditionally, and thus necessarily. An "infinite regression" is not possible. Kant objects that this impossibility is not given in the concept of causality itself. There is nothing in the concept of causality that compels us to conclude the series and to posit an ultimate (first) cause. Quite to the contrary! The principle entails that we continue to make different causal connections within the world to which the principle applies. If this process could be concluded, then the practice of *science* would come to an end. Scientific exploration presupposes that the causal chain is open-ended.[27] If one lets oneself be carried away by the ambiguous dynamic of reason to unconditionality and an all-encompassing totality, if by way of the principle of causality one arrives at the existence of an unconditional and necessary being on the other side of the world of experience, then reason runs aground in an aporia. How can we avoid the question concerning the one who is from all eternity: *"But whence then am I?"* One cannot resist this question and yet at the same time it is unbearable.[28]

What the cosmological proof has in mind—namely, stopping the regression—will turn out to be unable to withstand the remarkable dynamic of reason which both seeks to posit a closing term as well as break open every posited closure. Herein lies a reference to one of the positive meanings which, according to Kant, lies in the God of philosophy. We turn to this in the following section. It concerns what Kant calls the *ideas* of reason.

The Well-Ordered Cosmos—For Kant the pure concept of the most perfect being turns out not to open up a way to God. Even less is it possible on the basis of the unqualified experience of existence as such. Is there not at least one or other very specific experience which can lead to the affirmation of God?[29]

In any case, such an experience is found in what is traditionally called the *physico-theological* proof. Kant believes that this proof deserves our respect. It is the oldest, the clearest, and the most adapted to common sense. The decisive experience in this proof has to do with the order, the cohesion, and the purposiveness of nature.

Kant evokes this experience in the following terms.[30] The world opens for us a scene of plenitude, order, purposiveness, and beauty. No matter how far we explore space or penetrate the smallest pieces of matter, we are confronted everywhere by a remarkable cohesion. Every language falls short of adequately expressing the overwhelming impression made on us by the beautiful form of things and this perfect order. Everywhere we encounter an ingenious chain of cause and effect, of ends and means, of regularities in becoming and ceasing to be. Nothing has spontaneously come to be in the present condition it now exists. Everything always refers to something else, as to its condition of possibility. So one finally comes to the highest, or the ultimate condition of possibility of this well-ordered and purposive cohesion. As the highest teleological cause of everything, it unites all perfection in itself. The experience of order and purposiveness thus refers to a highest being which is the free and intelligent ground of the "cosmos."

Kant distinguishes four steps in the traditional physico-theological argument. First: everywhere in the world there are obvious signs of an order which is executed according to a specific purpose, and with great wisdom. Second step: this order is not inherent in the things of the world themselves. It is only contingently proper to them and is thus not generated by the nature of the things themselves. It can only be understood from a rational principle which forms the harmony and cohesion between things according to certain ideas. Third step: thus there exists one (or more) superior and wise cause. This cause is the cause of all that is, not in the way of a blind power producing everything, but in the way of an intelligent being that acts freely. Finally, the fourth step: the unity of this cause follows from the cohesion formed by the interplay of the parts of the world. One concludes to this, with certainty regarding the things we perceive, and with probability, according to the principles of analogy, concerning what transcends our perception.

As already mentioned, Kant had quite some sympathy for this proof. Nevertheless, he judges that this proof is also unable to lead to an apodictic affirmation of God's existence.

An initial reason for this lies in the analogy, utilized by the proof, between natural objects and artifacts. Artifacts presuppose an intelligent being as their cause. But from this it does not yet follow, at least not with apodictic certainty, that this must also be the case with natural things. With artifacts one knows from experience that they presuppose a maker. The principle of causality can here be validly applied because we are dealing with experiential data. This is not the case with natural objects. One cannot achieve any more certainty than is given by an argument from analogy.

Elsewhere, in the *Critique of Judgment,* Kant states that a purely mechanical explanation of the order and purposiveness in nature cannot be excluded in an apodictic manner. It is however impossible to fully realize this explanation, so that the reflective faculty of judgment justifiably calls upon the principle of finality.

But there is more that is problematic in the proof. Strictly speaking the proof merely lets us conclude a world architect (*Weltbaumeister*) and not a world creator. The analogy with the human artifact only leads to the principle of form. Human art only entails the purposive transformation of *given material* and not the origination of the artifact in all its aspects. The artifact is not a creation out of nothing. In this way the God of the physico-theological proof is not the cause of the substance of things. If one wanted to prove this, one would have to show that the purposive order is possible only because natural things are entirely the creation of the most perfect being. But for that purpose the argument from analogy to human art is too weak a basis.

The final weakness of the physico-theological proof appears to be the fact that it implicitly presupposes the validity of the cosmological proof. The order and purposiveness of the world are the point of departure, *the basis of experience*. This order appears to be so great and ingenious that it can only be explained by accepting a cause. What statements about this cause does the proof allow us? Experience allows us only to speak of a very great wisdom and intelligence. It does not permit us to conclude to a being "who possesses all might, wisdom . . . in a word, all the perfection proper to an all-sufficient being."[31]

The proof does something like this. It indeed wants to affirm the existence of God who, as including all reality, is understood as the most perfect being. But against this, Kant says that experience only lets us conclude to something very great, immeasurably powerful, and intelligent. That is something only *relatively* determined, that is to say, only in relation to us, but not in itself. The predicates "very great," "very intelligent," and so on, are only relative predicates. They do not determine the being as it is in itself, but only as it is in relation to us. But the concept of an absolutely perfect being is the concept of a being completely determined in itself. The experiential basis falls short of reaching that end. Thus for Kant there is no empirical route from the experience of the world's order and purposiveness to God. Only a speculative way is possible. This way, however, is invalid.

The *physico-theological* proof takes experience as its starting point. When this falls short it shifts over to an argument from the principle of contingency, thus to the *cosmological* proof. But earlier on, this was shown to be invalid because at a crucial moment it covers up its inadequacy by switching over to the *ontological* proof.

Kant concludes his refutation of the classical proofs with the following consideration:

> Thus the physico-theological proof of the existence of an original or supreme being rests upon the cosmological proof, and the cosmological

upon the ontological . . . and since, besides these three, there is no other path open to speculative reason, the ontological proof from pure concepts of reason is the only possible one.[32]

This unavoidable presence of the ontological argument entails, and this has been thoroughly demonstrated, that the whole speculative construction is groundless.

In the traditional proofs for the existence of God, reason succumbs to the temptation to transgress the limits to which it is inherently bound. As we will see shortly, what may "only" be interpreted as an ideal of reason, is unjustifiably affirmed as an objectively existing actuality.

3.2 THE SCOPE OF THE CRITIQUE

It Concerns the Entirety of a Philosophy—In truth, the expression "proof for the existence of God" is not felicitous. It suggests that one could know who or what God is prior to, and independently of, the thinking contained in, the proof. The philosophical concept of God is comprehensible only as a *result*. This means it requires proper attention to the experiences of thought that structure the proof. What Hegel says about philosophical truth is applicable here: it *is* only as a result. Apart from the way leading to it, and thus taken separately, it is merely an *assertion* (or *assurance*) or a religious conviction which draws its truth from other experiences.

Moreover, "proof" is ill-suited because it creates the impression that one is merely dealing with a specific branch of a philosophy, a component which would exist relatively independent of the rest. In truth, and against all appearances, in the "proof" or in its critique, an entire philosophy, along with its leading principles, is unified and brought to a final expression. At issue is the fundamental metaphysical position that every philosophy assumes. The discourse concerning the Absolute is more than a branch of a particular philosophy. It is rather the exposition of the final position taken up in a philosophy with respect to truth and actuality.

We should not be misled by the form of this "proof," namely as a separate chapter (such as: Anselm's *Proslogion*, Descartes' *third* and *fifth meditation*, and so on). While the Absolute can be explicitly thematized in a particular branch of a philosophy, given its proper nature, it must be understood as alpha and omega: it concerns *all*. This also holds for Kant's philosophy. To gauge accurately the scope of his critique, it is important to bear this in mind.

We must pursue in greater depth the leading presuppositions of the critique, as well as its architectonic context: its place and function within the entirety of Kant's philosophy.

The ideal of pure reason—The immediate context of Kant's critique is the third chapter of the second book of the *Transcendental Dialectic* in the *Critique of Pure Reason*. The chapter is entitled *The ideal of pure reason*. With this chapter, Kant concludes his considerations about the transcendental dialectic. In *The Transcendental Dialectic* Kant explicitly develops his critique of metaphysics, in so far as this is understood as pure theoretical knowledge of the supersensible. Such knowledge wholly exceeds the phenomenal reality given in experience. It bears upon metaphysical "objects" such as the I, the world, and God. Kant claims that metaphysics is not something fortuitous. Metaphysics is necessarily related to the essence of reason. Reason contains within itself an unappeasable desire to arrive at the highest unity of what the understanding offers to us. At stake is the systematic unity of all experience. This unity functions as the ultimate horizon of what appears. It is with the unconditional that our longing for knowledge and insight comes to rest. At the same time, Kant shows that reason, in traditional metaphysical practice, entangles itself in a *logic of mere appearance*. Dialectic is no longer, as for example in Aristotle, that which only yields "probable" knowledge. It merely yields a *semblance of knowledge* and not valid theoretical knowledge of the supersensible.

In the section on the *Ideal of Reason* all this is applied to the most general, comprehensive, absolutely unconditional, and highest idea of metaphysics—namely, God. What does it mean, that in thinking God metaphysics necessarily entangles itself in a logic of mere appearance?[33] To clarify this it is necessary to elucidate the specific status of the idea of God.

Like the other ideas, such as the I and the world, the idea of God brings unity and cohesion to the knowledge that is expressed on the categorical level in judgments. The idea of God fulfills this function, as it were, in the most radical manner. The idea of the *I* provides the ultimate, unconditional unity and ground of all *representations*. It represents the I as the ultimate subject, which itself can no longer be a predicate of a subject, "the absolute (unconditioned) unity of the thinking subject." The idea of the *world* indicates the absolute unity of the conditions of *phenomena*, "the absolute unity of the series of conditions of appearance." Where the I is the ground of the subjective unity (absolute subject) and the world is the ground of the objective unity (absolute object), the *idea of God is "the absolute unity of the condition of all objects of thought in general."*[34]

God is therefore the most encompassing metaphysical idea. Hence, Kant names the idea of God the *transcendental ideal* of reason. He thus expresses the distinction between the idea of God and the categories of the understanding and the other ideas. The categories have a direct bearing on sensibly given phenomena. This is not so with the ideas. The ideas refer to a supersensible actuality. The ideas of the I and the world, nevertheless, maintain a certain connection with the world of experiences, in any case more than does the idea of God. The idea of God appears to be furthest removed from the world of the senses. Kant writes: "But what I entitle the *ideal* seems further removed from the objective reality even than the idea. By the ideal I understand the idea, not merely *in concreto*, but *in individuo*, that is, as an individual thing, determinable or even determined by the idea alone."[35]

By way of illustration, Kant refers to Plato. The idea of humanity, for example, is unique and contains all possible human perfection. That is why it is an ideal. However, only concerning God, Kant holds, does one rightly speak of an ideal. It is the ultimate and most encompassing condition of possibility of all that is. The idea of God contains the total possibility of all conceivable beings: *omnitudo realitatis*. It surpasses everything. It does this because it is a condition, and in this it still resembles the other ideas. But it lies higher and further than the other ideas; that is why it is called the ideal; it is the idea of the most perfect being that completely transcends every experience.

How does reason arrive at the construction of this Ideal? The key here is what Kant calls *durchgängige Bestimmung* (complete determination). All that exists is so and not otherwise: it is determined, characterized by specific predicates which make it this specific thing, distinguished from all other things. A thing cannot contain contradictory predicates: it cannot, for example, be at the same time and in the same respect both dead and alive, here and not here. In order to be completely determined, one of each opposed predicates must always belong to that thing. But this means that each being can only be considered completely determined in relation to a being which contains all possible predicates within itself. Kant writes: "The proposition, *everything which exists is completely determined*, does not mean only that one of every pair of *given* contradictory predicates, but that one of every [pair of] *possible* predicates, must always belong to it."[36] But this means, continues Kant, that in order to fully know something "we must know every possible [predicate], and must determine it thereby, either affirmatively or negatively."[37]

Nothing can be completely determined without a relation to an absolutely perfect being that represents the unity of all real and conceivable predicates. The situation is equivalent to wanting to determine someone's positive and negative value. Such an endeavor only succeeds by way of comparing the person with an ideal which possesses all possible perfections. Of course, this complete determination cannot be executed *in concreto*, because this would entail covering the totality of all possible predicates.

Nevertheless, if something is affirmed as existing, then we assume such complete determination. This implies that reason constructs a substance or substratum whose essence is to contain all predicates. It contains all *realitas* in itself. The point here is the realization of all perfection in one individual being. This is God. God is, as it were, the entire store of the material from which all possible predicates of things are supplied.

Kant formulates this as follows:

All possibility of things . . . must therefore be regarded as derivative, with only one exception, namely, the possibility of that which includes in itself all reality. This latter possibility must be regarded as original. For all negations (which are the only predicates through which anything can be distinguished from the *ens realissimum*) are merely limitations of a greater, and ultimately of the highest, reality; and they therefore presuppose this reality, and are, as regards their content, derived from it. All manifoldness of things is only a correspondingly varied mode of limiting the concept of the highest reality which forms their common substratum, just as all figures are only possible as so many different modes of limiting infinite space. The object of the ideal of reason, an object which is only present to us in and through reason, is therefore entitled the *primordial being (ens originarium)* . . . the *highest being (ens summum)*, and . . . the *being of all beings (ens entium)*."[38]

All negative predicates refer back to that *ens summum*, because they are all derivative: every negation is conceivable only if it is grounded in the opposite affirmation. This *ens realissimum* is completely determined. From all the pairs of contradictory predicates the *ens realissimum* contains that which expresses the *realitas* (the negation are privations, thus they do not affect the most perfect being). Because the highest being unifies all possible predicates in itself, the ideal must also be thought, according to Kant, as characterized by personhood and intelligence. This ideal is the ultimate condition of possibility which reason *must think*, to be able to give an explanation of what it truly knows. Here God does not appear as an external *deus ex machina* who is brought in from elsewhere, for example, from religion. Rather, God is the end-term of a process which thought undergoes when it wants to comprehend its *knowing* of actuality.

Kant rejects every possibility of affirming the *existence of the absolute*—this is sufficiently evident in the above. As with the other ideas, the ideal has only a *regulative* character. Unlike the categories of understanding, the ideal does not have a constitutive function. Together with the matter given in sensible intuition, the categories form what is the object of objective rational knowledge. As is well known, valid theoretical knowledge is always reliant on something given in experience. This is not the case with what is thought in the ideas. The

I, the world, and God, are not given in sensible intuition. They do not give objective knowledge, and they do not refer to objects that appear. As Kant writes: "I understand by idea a necessary concept of reason to which no corresponding object can be given in sense-experience."[39] An object which is adequate to the transcendental idea can never appear in experience. So the world as the totality of all phenomena is never given to us; all that is given is this or that phenomenon that belongs to the world. Ideas are therefore not *given in knowing*. These pure concepts of reason must be considered as a *task* for *thought*: "[they] are thus at least necessary as setting us the task of extending the unity of understanding, where possible, up to the unconditioned."[40] When we do not see this (and this for Kant is the error of traditional dogmatic metaphysics) we become ensnared in transcendental illusion. In this transcendental illusion ideas are presented as something which provide us with knowledge of certain objects.

The Positive Turn—The unmasking of this illusion does not as such lead to the elimination of ideas, but to a redefinition of their essence and function. Their function is regulative instead of constitutive:

> Transcendental ideas never allow of any constitutive employment . . . .
> On the other hand, they have an excellent, and indeed indispensably necessary, regulative employment, namely, that of directing the understanding toward a certain goal upon which the routes marked out by all its rules converge, as upon their point of intersection. This point is indeed a mere idea, a *focus imaginarius*, from which, since it lies quite outside the bounds of possible experience, the concepts of the understanding do not in reality proceed; none the less it serves to give to these concepts the greatest [possible] unity combined with the greatest [possible] extension.[41]

I offer this long citation because it is an excellent expression of Kant's position.

The ideas represent something that is included in the nature of rational knowing—namely, the unconditional unity of all experiential knowing. That is why the movement from reason to the ideas is rooted in a subjective necessity, and not guaranteed by an objective reality.

This does not make the ideas redundant, or into a merely speculative game. The ideas are of essential significance for experiential knowing. As regulative, they can be considered as a sort of guideline in the methodically organized process of (scientific) knowing. They represent the *whole*, which itself can never become the object of knowledge, but which energizes each concrete knowing toward more and more new knowledge. One can look upon them as the intellectual conditions of the possibility of science, where science is understood as a never-ending process. This applies par excellence to the idea of God, the ideal of the ultimate unconditional unity of all our knowing.

From this the *unmasking* of the transcendental illusion takes on a *positive meaning*. The unveiling only affects the ontological status of the ideas. When applied to the idea of God this means that God can neither be affirmed nor denied. The idea of God is *problematic*, which for Kant means: "If the objective reality of a concept cannot be in any way known, while yet the concept contains no contradiction . . . I entitle that concept problematic."[42] What cannot be decided is problematic. The existence of God can neither be confirmed nor denied.

And so the critique of the proofs for God and the designation of the limits of (theoretical) reason also have a positive meaning. Every dogmatic atheism is excluded. Moreover, although problematic, the idea of God is nevertheless a consistent idea. Kant speaks of a *flawless ideal (fehlerfreies Ideal)*.[43]

This means that the entire line of thinking must now be directed toward the problematic of existence. Kant himself writes that once the problem of existence is solved—thus he alludes to the ethical way, Kant's "own way," discussed below—the theoretical idea of God can fulfil a prominent role.[44] It can exert a critical and purifying function. It can arm against all possible forms of anthropomorphism, deism, or superstition. It can prevent one from confusing the absolute with one or another being affected by sensibility, for this "is out of keeping with the supreme reality."[45]

Kant's critique of the traditional proofs has become classic. The danger is that it begins to function as something self-evident, something barely appropriated in a productive manner. One cannot adequately judge this critique unless one includes the doctrine of the ideal of reason. This can lead to the following considerations.

The distance which separates Kant from the tradition is smaller than would appear at first sight. Just as for Anselm, for Thomas, for Descartes, and for many others, God is linked with a certain *experience which thought undergoes*. The transcendental project necessarily implies a movement of reason toward the Unconditional. The essential appears to be something that becomes present in a thinking that tries to go to the limit of its possibilities. Having reached its limits, thought touches something which simultaneously surpasses thought. Higher than the ideal, there is nothing more to think. Though it is constructed in thought, at the same time the ideal seems to surpass the faculty of cognition. This transcendence emerges in Kant's reservation with respect to the affirmation of God's existence. This reservation does not make the concept of God into a phantom, a phantasm, or an impossible chimera. Though the objective existence of the concept of God cannot be theoretically affirmed, it is nevertheless a *meaningful* actuality. With respect to its content, the connection between Kant's concept of God and that maintained in the tradition is clear, of course. Indeed, God is also thought by Kant as the most perfect being, the origin of all actuality: *omnitudo realitatis*. The concept of God must not only be called meaningful. Concerning reason's interest in complete knowledge, the concept of God is also necessary.

All this does not alter the fact that God remains a *subjective* concept (for theoretical reason). In the last section of this chapter I will ask about the meaning of Kant's remarkable reserve regarding the affirmation of God's existence.

But first I take up Kant's own solutions to that problem, Kant's "own way": the postulation of God's existence out of *ethical experience*.

3.3 KANT'S WAY: THE ABSOLUTENESS OF THE OUGHT

It has become a popular tale. It comes from Heinrich Heine. Kant's first critique had an unbelievably destructive effect. It deprived humankind of all his attachments and everything that provided his life with a solid base. Kant realized that his old and loyal manservant Lampe could not live in such an agnostic climate. "Old Lampe must have a God, otherwise the poor man cannot be happy."[46] Hence the *Critique of Practical Reason.*

It is just a story. The kernel of truth it contains is that the affirmation of the existence of what is called the ideal of reason is only possible through a shift in perspective. The possibility of affirming God is not based on consideration of nature, but of *freedom* and the *morality* based upon it. It looks as if in Kant the first effect of the desacralization by the sciences—namely, the dedivinization of nature—receives a philosophical interpretation. Nature is reduced to what falls within the horizon of the empirical and its mathematical explanation.

The only place for an affirmation of God now seems to be the *human being.* Not the human being as a being of nature, but precisely insofar as he is withdrawn from the power of nature as a moral and free being. That the essential is no fiction but must be affirmed as present, emerges, for Kant, from a reflection on the implications of moral "experience."[47]

After Kant this way will not be undertaken with such force and conviction, except perhaps by Emmanuel Levinas. However, Levinas's ethical metaphysics rather leads to a sort of negative theology, and thus, in a certain sense, comes into the vicinity of the logic of absence.[48]

From the nineteenth century the human and social sciences will radically change the world of experience, as the natural sciences had done previously with respect to the perception of nature. The human being and society will more and more be conceived within the "compelling" framework of empiricism and quantity.

Their self-evident reference to a divine actuality will disappear, even where people will continue to stress, in opposition to all sorts of reductionism, the irreducibility of what is specifically human. Practical philosophy will lose its theological implications. Ethics will more and more refer to ethics, and humanity to humanity itself.

With Kant, on the contrary, autonomy and the affirmation of God are still linked to each other. From the second half of the nineteenth century, they are mostly separated from each other and assigned to diverse spheres. On the one hand, there is the sphere of the rationally argued universal morality. On the other hand, there is the sphere of the personal meaning of life, and eventually of religion. Faith in God and autonomy will sometimes even be presented as irreconcilable.[49]

The peculiar road taken by Kant is particularly interesting against this background. Without in any way weakening the principle of autonomy, he develops a perspective on the Absolute out of ethics. For Kant, God is not a condition for morality. God is not a motive which would confer a moral value on our actions. God is not something we would have to affirm lest the whole world of norms and values should collapse. God is not something after which we strive in our moral actions as a sort of highest good. Nor does God respond to a kind of moral need. All these forms of infringement on the principle of autonomy are opposed to the fundamental principles of ethics.

In our analysis of Kant's "own way," of course, we limit ourselves to the essential. Two things are foremost: first, the link between autonomy and the affirmation of God; second, the problem of existence already under discussion in the doctrine of the *Ideal of Reason*.[50]

The Indisputable Moral "Fact"—In a footnote in T*he Critique of Practical Reason* Kant writes that his moral philosophy does not aim to construct a new kind of morality.[51] The philosopher must not act as if before him the world had no idea of what is morally required. Moral philosophy is not primarily a construction, but a clarification of what is given with existence as such. This is expressed very clearly in what Kant calls the fact of reason, *Faktum der Vernunft*.

The human being stands essentially under the imperative of an unconditional duty. An awareness of this imperative imposes itself *nolens volens*. One does not derive such an unconditional duty from long theoretical explorations. This duty is neither hypothetical nor merely probable. No, Kant chooses precisely the term *Faktum* to indicate the *apodictic* character proper to the consciousness of standing under moral duty.

The point here is a very special kind of facticity. This facticity does not fall under empirical intuition. It is not to be ascertained as any natural phenomenon or as any particular behavior. It concerns the fact of an ought, of something that "should" (*Sollen*) be. The term *Faktum* emphasizes the incontrovertible manner in which the ethical imperative importunes. For example, one knows immediately that there is a qualitative difference between deceiving someone and making a mistake when giving someone information. To illustrate the clarity and unconditionality with which the ethical *ought* manifests itself, Kant provides a well-chosen example in the *Critique of Practical Reason*. The example shows all the elements necessary to silence this fact.[52] Suppose someone declares that in a certain situation his desire for pleasure is truly irresistible. Could not this person easily overcome his desire, if he were absolutely certain that it would cost him his life: certain death after getting pleasure? But now imagine the same person in the following situation. Under threat of immediate and certain execution, his sovereign forces him to bear false witness against someone, and thus to cause the ruin of an honest and innocent man. Perhaps, Kant continues, he would not dare guarantee what actually he will or will not do. Yet, if questioned, he will promptly admit that he considers it possible to remain true to the command to speak the truth. "He judges," writes Kant, "that he can do something because he knows he *ought* (*soll*), and he recognizes that he is free—a fact which, without the moral law, would have remained unknown to him."[53]

The gallows, which is stronger than the tendency for voluptuousness, is not stronger than the command to speak the truth. Central to Kant's example is the absolute certainty with which the human being knows that he is not to bear false witness. It is irrelevant whether, in this particular case, the command of truthfulness will endure the power struggle with the threat of death. What reveals itself as an undeniable fact is the unconditional nature of an ought which here appears as in no way conditioned by the safety of one's life.

This moral experience reveals a very particular necessity, a necessity bound up with *freedom*. In his book *De immorele mens*, J. De Visscher gives a contemporary illustration of the point that Kant is making.[54] One can try to reconstruct the social-psychological antecedents which, at the time, led the American Lieutenant Calley to bring about such a gruesome blood bath in the Vietnamese village of My Lai. From a theoretical perspective we can make intelligible in large measure the fact that it "had to happen that way." But the logic of the development leading to this event cannot prevent one from still exclaiming: this cannot happen, this should not happen. This assessment indicates the specific logic of the moral law, as opposed to a quasi-naturally necessitated must.

In Kant, the evidence of this fact is not open to any doubt, not even the slightest hesitation. It is "graven into the human soul in the crudest, most legible script."[55]

The Postulate of God's Existence—The moral imperative of which one is conscious in the *Faktum* is autonomous. It is not conditioned by something else, not even by some religious conviction or a theistic worldview. Though the validity of the moral law does not depend upon accepting the existence of God, moral "experience" does lead, with Kant, to the conviction of God's existence. The existence of a highest being is postulated on the basis of morality. This being is conceived as the moral creator of the world, as the cause of both the natural and the moral order, and as the ground of phenomenality and noumenality.

Kant comes to this conclusion on the grounds of a very simple consideration. Central to this is what he calls the *highest good*.

Moral virtue is unconditionally good. Yet it is not the perfect and completed totality of the good.[56] What is missing is *happiness (Glückseligkeit)*: "The condition of a rational being in the world, in whose whole existence everything goes according to wish and will . . . rests on the harmony of nature with his whole end and with the essential determining ground of his will."[57]

The human being does not only stand under the unconditional ethical imperative. It is also a needy being who seeks satisfaction. The human being is in search of happiness. Then the *highest good* (highest in the sense of complete, *vollendet, consummatum*) lies, according to Kant, not surprisingly, in the unity of happiness and moral virtue. Given the character of the ethical good (to be highest in the sense of supreme, *oberst, supremum*), it is essential to this unity that happiness is in proportion to virtue.[58] This is expressed in the concept of one's *worthiness of happiness (Glückswürdigkeit)*. Only those who act morally make themselves worthy of happiness. Everyone can hope for that amount of happiness of which they have made themselves worthy in respect of their ethical excellence.

What does all this have to do with God?

According to Kant it is evident that the necessary synthesis of happiness and virtue is in no way guaranteed. The virtuous person is not always happy, on the contrary. Happiness does not depend entirely on ourselves. It is also dependent on natural circumstances and other factors beyond our control. Kant thinks that what does lie within our power is worthiness of happiness, not the highest good itself.

If this synthesis does not lie within our power and nevertheless is our highest aim, then this synthesis is only possible on the ground of another being that guarantees the proportional apportioning of happiness. Such a being must be *all-knowing* (in order to know the proportion), *all-mighty* (it must govern nature in order to realize the allocation), and absolutely *just* (a holy will which applies the principle of proportional allocation in a perfectly just manner). Kant thinks this being can only be *God*. As a just creator God is the principle of the moral law and the power over nature.

Kant calls this "proof" a *postulate*. He defines it as follows: "By a postulate of pure practical reason, I understand a theoretical proposition which is not as such demonstrable, but which is an inseparable corollary of an a priori unconditionally valid practical law."[59] Therefore, postulating is not the construction of some theoretical hypothesis. Postulates are not theoretical dogmas but presuppositions *(Voraussetzungen)* from a necessarily practical perspective. They do not amplify speculative knowledge but give objective reality and legitimacy to the ideas of speculative reason in general via their relation to the practical sphere.[60] Hence, instead of calling this knowledge theoretical knowledge, it is better to call it pure *rational faith (Vernunftglaube)*: reason is the source from which this faith springs.[61]

The certainty effected by the postulates is of a *subjective-practical* nature. It is something the subject, respecting obedience to the practical (moral) laws, "must" assume. Thus, postulating contains a very special combination of subjectivity and necessity. It can therefore be called a *necessary faith*.

Kant's "proof," his own way, is the philosophical translation of a general human existential-moral experience, albeit Kant's rather juridical framework hinders the explication of the full wealth of this experience. The course of the world and human fate often have an air of unacceptability, running counter to our sense of justice. This is the case, for instance, when we see that the innocent suffer and the guilty profit. Virtue often goes unrewarded and happiness is not always surrounded by morality. Yet the highest good remains the ultimate object of the will. For this orientation of the will not to be meaningless, its realization should be possible in one way or other. Here we find an analogous argument to the one Kant developed for freedom. No theoretical proof is possible for the affirmation of freedom. After all, we cannot see freedom. If we could see freedom then freedom would *eo ipso* be impossible: it would fall under the determinism proper to the phenomenal order. Nevertheless, we must affirm freedom from a practical point of view: "He judges . . . that he can do something because he knows that he ought."[62] If the ethical demand is not to be a purely unrealizable ought, the human being must possess the means for its realization. Otherwise ethical desire would be no more than a kind of *passion inutile* (useless passion).[63]

In all this there are two essential issues. First, the unquestionable truth and originality of the ethical experience. This is for Kant truly a *fait primitif* (primitive fact). The human being is a moral being who is not indifferent to what is true and good. Consequently reason necessitates certain assumptions without which this *ought* cannot be deemed fully meaningful. Kant's practical faith in reason is the realization of what is proper to philosophy as such: "faith" in the rationality of actuality. In the following chapters I will take a closer look at the experience of evil and suffering which put this rationality to the test.

The orientation toward the absolute is not only implied in the problematic of the proportioned allocation of happiness. The unconditional nature of the moral law posits the human being in a remarkable relation. One the one hand, there is the complete autonomy of the moral law. In the moral law we are obedient to a law of (pure) practical reason, and not to an external, heteronomous authority. On the other hand, this autonomy is in no way Promethean. The human being is not only a legislator, but also a subject in the realm of ends. This means that the moral law also appears with a mark of radical *transcendence*. An essential feature of the ethical experience is the awareness that the good and the just are not things at our arbitrary disposal. We all stand under the ethical idea in an equal manner. Ethics confronts us with an absolute, with something that we ourselves do not constitute. It refers to a noumenal realm of goodness and justice. It *refers* to the actuality of all perfection and to the actuality of what theoretical reason, in the *Ideal of Reason*, could only declare problematic.

This reference must take place without committing a "category mistake." The Ideal does not hereby become an objectively "known" actuality. God remains a postulate.

3.4 THE LIMITS OF THE LIMITS

Kant's critique has become classic. For some this means that it has become definitive. Yet now, as in the past, this critique appears to be itself the object of critique. There is an impressive tradition of critique of the critique. The history of this tradition cannot be adequately dealt with here. I limit myself to a few systematic considerations. These considerations regard important presuppositions in Kant's thought. Attention to these presuppositions can relativize the absoluteness of the limits which Kant thought he must draw. In a second moment I will focus on the fundamental metaphysical élan of Kant's thought.

Critique of the Critique—Since Kant's critique, philosophical talk concerning God has definitely lost all its naivety. Perhaps what is most important about this critique is its *therapeutic* effect—namely, to guard philosophy against zealotries (against becoming *schwärmerisch,* as Kant would say), or against losing oneself in wild speculations. This mistrust of unfounded claims to reason need not be paralyzing. To speak with Hegel, it need not prevent a mistrust of this mistrust.[64] This implies among other things that we must gauge what remains *irreflechie* in Kant's philosophy but which still in a certain sense determines his thought. The point is to put the presuppositions and conditions of possibility of Kant's philosophy under "prior scrutiny" (*vorher zu prüfen*), to cite Hegel once more.[65]

Furthermore, concerning the philosophical problem of God, it is important to interpret Kant's now classic critique of the proofs within the context of his entire philosophy. I have already mentioned that the *Ideal of Reason* nuances Kant's critique in an important sense. To a degree, it expresses the experiences of thought which I have interpreted as ways to God in the second chapter. In these experiences reason, because of its own dynamic, comes to something absolute. Of course, in the *Ideal of Reason* Kant does not speak of *experiences of thought*. The term "experience" has too limited a range in Kant's philosophy. For Kant, *experience* refers to a form of knowing which remains essentially bound to sensible intuition (although knowledge is not reduced to it). It does not have as ample a meaning as it will have in Hegel or later in hermeneutics. The term seems modeled after the way knowing operates in the natural sciences. What is expressed in the experiences of thought I discussed is not excluded, but comes back, as it were, in another "language game." When it delves into the last presuppositions of knowing, when it reaches the limit of its possibilities, *thought* (not knowledge) finds itself necessarily thinking *something that is absolute*.

Thought, of course, is not able to affirm the *existence* of this absolute (neither can it deny its existence). It remains, as it were, helplessly suspended (*im Schweben*).[66] But it is also true that in the experience of thought I developed, the process does not terminate in the affirmation of a *being*. On the contrary, thought experiences that it must affirm something radically transcending ordinary categorical structures. God is not thought as a being among beings, but as the *ground* of all beings, as the perfection of all perfections, as the one in which essence and existence coincide, as the *ideatum* which endlessly surpasses the idea we have of it. The affirmation of being to which thought comes in no way entails the being-there of something over and against a subject. What is at stake here is more than a "Position."

God's being is not thought as analogous to the existence of an objectivity over and against a subjectivity. The affirmation of being does not fit into the common subject-object opposition. That is why Kant's famous distinction between a hundred imagined talers and a hundred existing talers is somewhat misleading. Hegel has sharply protested against this point. Naturally, something is not yet actual just because I represent it to myself. Anyone can see this. Hence the success of Kant's critique of the ontological proof. It does not require much labor of thought! But according to Hegel, Kant's critique does not strike the heart of the matter.[67] When we speak about God the point is not some indifferent concept or representation. The distance between a hundred talers and God is infinite. It is characteristic of all finite beings that their existence is distinguished from their concept. In God, however, something is thought in which this nonidentity is sublated. The unity of concept and being precisely constitutes the concept of God.

Hegel's critique of Kant starts from a different frame of reference—namely, the fundamental *unity of thought and being*. In Kant's Copernican turn the concept threatens to lose its ontological anchoring and become a subjective mode of thought. *Being* is reduced to an objectivity over and against a subjectivity: *Position eines Dinges*.

On the one hand, Kant's critique continues what implicitly holds in the tradition I have discussed—namely, that the affirmation of God is not to be understood as the affirmation of a being within the usual categorical structures. On the other hand, Kant seems unable to give a positive turn to this reservation. The gap between thought and being stands in the way of this. Kant does not take full advantage of the gain of a valid critique of a dogmatic metaphysics. Kant's own doctrine of the transcendental ideal of reason especially offered an opportunity.

That this opportunity was not taken is due, to a large extent, to the hegemony of the *understanding* (*Verstand*) through which the unifying élan of reason was partially broken. What will become the dominant thought after Kant (with the exception of German idealism)—namely, the collapse of a broader rationality into empiricism and a formal logic of the understanding—appears to be rooted in Kant's philosophy itself.

If reason attempts to be more than just subservient to an understanding bound to sensible intuition, then it becomes *dialectical*.[68] According to Kant, this dialectic entails that reason, no longer held by the constraints of the sensible world and developing itself further solely by means of its own concepts, entangles itself in *contradictions*. It can then no longer offer real knowledge. On purely rational grounds and with equal right, we could claim, for example, that the world is finite as well as infinite; that it has neither end nor beginning in time and space; that every substance is divisible and that this is not the case. This is the same dialectic that is the object of critique in Kant's treatment of the cosmological proof. On the one hand, we must state that there is an absolutely necessary highest being which is the ultimate ground of all things (among other reasons, to avoid an infinite regress). On the other hand, we cannot resist doing the exact opposite, and again asking about that being: Where does it come from (*"aber woher ben ich denn?"*).[69]

What becomes manifest here is the transcendental illusion that is bound up with this dialectic. The thought of a highest being as absolutely necessary cancels itself out. After all it refers to the possibility of further questioning, into infinity. Reason is divided within itself. It is as much directed toward closing off its fundamental movement as it cannot be satisfied with any closure. Kant solves this problem by ascribing a purely *regulative* meaning to reason. The ambiguous dynamic of both conclusive explanation and questioning that goes further and further, is realized in scientific practice.

Reason, its regulative function, supplies the methodological rules for this practice. Reason is thus restricted to the phenomenal domain and detached from actuality as it is in itself. Reason loses its ontological range. Kant thus only thematized the necessity of the dialectic in a limited sense. His analysis primarily has a negative meaning.

The limitation of reason's immanent dialectic appears predominantly in contrast with Hegel's interpretation. Hegel reproaches Kant for unreflectively thinking in terms of the prejudices of the tradition. There *being* is understood as an abstract identity which is without contradiction. That is why Kant is forced to lay all contradictions on the side of *reason*. But then God cannot be known, because reason can only think God as something that is in itself contradictory.

In contrast to this view Hegel will value this contradiction *positively*. The *dialectic* is not just something in our (subjective) thought but, because the fundamental unity of thought and being, it is *a feature of actuality itself*. God cannot be understood as a separate being or as an abstract objectivity. God is *Spirit*, the highest Spirit, which is to say that God is an actuality which is unity-in-difference: the unity that is one *in* the contradiction of distinguishing itself from itself. Perhaps this is the only adequate answer to Kant's critique. The transcendental illusion becomes itself illusion when thought realizes that the *contradictions* which it generates belong *to God*.

Therefore God cannot be understood according to the model of objective being. Understanding cannot attain to God because it can only reach objects. Only reason can come to the affirmation of God. God is then the *Absolute* and not a being alongside or beyond finite beings but "the unique *principium essendi* and *cognoscendi*" of all that is.[70]

The Metaphysical Élan—Kant has not succeeded in fully ascribing positive value to the speculative power that lies hidden in his thought. This holds particularly for what he writes about the ideal of reason, and the transcendental apperception, and for the synthesis which is presented in the *Critique of Judgment*.

This remains somewhat enigmatic. As will have become clear from my elucidation, Kant's critique of metaphysics is in no way motivated toward making finitude absolute. Kant's critique of a philosophical concept of God is in no way inspired by atheism or agnosticism. On the contrary, his philosophy explicates in its own way what is essential for the experiences of thought that lead to the affirmation of God—namely, *openness to transcendence*. Kant's criticism not only problematizes dogmatic metaphysics: *it limits the claims of an exclusively scientific rationality*. This critique of a scientific rationality which does not respect its limits, "that would be everything," opens a space for freedom and thus for transcendence. Kant's decisiveness in formulating the metaphysical and "theological" relevance of ethical experience, is one of the most notable aspects of his thought. There is no need for a critique of *pure* practical reason, because pure practical reason is not under threat of transcendental illusion.

Indeed, Kant's critique also has an *ontological* ground. The principles of practical philosophy not only focus attention on reasonable coherence or abstract universality. The "you ought" of the categorical imperative points to a *being* which *resists* every form of instrumentalization, or appropriation, or utilization: the human being as the bearer of the moral law. The human being is an actuality which cannot be produced or constructed, but which is to be *respected* in its independence. Ethical experience is the experience of an actuality which is to be respected "unconditionally" and which as independent sets limits. What is at issue here is a privileged experience of *being*, and of inescapable *presence* of something that does not evaporate under the power of our projects. This experience allows us to see what scientific and technological rationality which seems able to do almost "anything," really is—namely, *finite*.

Naturally, with this God is not given. The absoluteness of the ethical does not presuppose the affirmation of God. The moral imperative holds as it is and is not conditioned by God. Still, for a thinking which tries to understand this absoluteness of the ethical, it can be a reference to the Ground of the ethical. Nevertheless, this movement which would go "further" and which thought *can* undergo, remains very precarious. This is so not only from the central perspective of this chapter (namely, the theoretical perspective) but also, and perhaps especially, from the point of view of more existential experiences. These are precisely connected with the value of human beings *as* human beings, and concern forms of *suffering* and *evil*.

What might be the meaning of this shadowy side of our existence for a philosophical reflection on God?

4
Auschwitz: The End of an Illusion?

4.1 THE MYSTERY OF EVIL

Beyond any Concept?—*"Car comment une seule larme—fut-elle effacée—pourrait s'oublier?"* ("for how could one sole tear—though it be effaced—be forgotten?).[1]

These words of Levinas describe in a unique manner how deeply suffering encroaches on our existence. They highlight our impotence to undo what has happened. But they say more. They also express a value judgment: "the pain that glints in a tear . . ." need not be.[2] This pain reveals something to be broken, uprooted, or destroyed; what was whole falls apart; what carried within itself the promise to grow into something, is blocked.

Being has a mysterious shadow-side which shows itself in the different forms of our suffering: bodily pain and decay, breakdown, loss, psychological suffering, despair, suffocating hopelessness, grief in many forms, sickness, death.

This shadow-side is mysterious. It is as essential as light, unmistakably present and ineradicable. At the same time, however, it is experienced as something that properly—ideally?—need not be. The shadow becomes an impenetrable mystery when it falls on what is most properly our own: our will, our disposition; *mysterium iniquitatis*: the mystery of evil, injustice, of the pain and suffering to which we subject ourselves and others.

It seems that the deeper evil lies within our ownmost I, the more obstinate it becomes. The more it belongs to us, the less it seems to be under our self-control and the more it strikes us as an unfathomable, incomprehensible, and strange fate. What is said of death—that it withdraws itself as a mystery: *ultima latet* (the ultimate remains hidden)[3]—also holds for evil in its typically human form, moral evil, for all suffering and pain that is connected with our will. The mystery of evil is: the injustice, the humiliation, the lie, the brute violence or the refined subjugation of torture, the cold eye that objectifies, takes stock, and strikes.

A few years ago, in a unique film—*Shoah*—Claude Lanzmann "showed" the annihilation of the Jews in the Nazi death camp. The film contains nothing fictional. It is a kind of documentary reconstruction. The camera shows places where camps stood, rails on which the trains carrying the Jews entered the camps, documents in which the *Endlösung* was organized, and faces and voices of the victims who survived, of camp executioners, of those who were responsible, of bystanders. The sound track records what appears to be impossible: speaking about what the images suggest (not "show"). The cracking of a voice that threatens to approach the unspeakable. The long silences. The cautious reaching for words to speak the unutterable without twisting or nullifying it. The numerous betrayals of unbelievable emotions in a change of subject, a glance, a look in the eyes, a gesture, a word, a hesitation. No documentary commentary accompanies the images. Only an attempt at saying that here it is almost impossible to speak. The film shows people who have barely survived, who have taken part, who were unable to help others or did not want to, who are more or less responsible, or who coolly tried to save what there was to save. All voices, faces, gestures of people who experienced it, who have been touched by the dark side of our being: the mystery of evil.

There is nothing exciting or sensational in the film. You do not cry while watching it. It does however leave you in a strange confusion and you are overwhelmed by unplaceable feelings and moods. What is shown is like death, of which we say: *ultima latet*.

The attempt to understand what is shown seems to come to a standstill.

An analogous experience can be had by visiting one of the camp blocks at Auschwitz. One can, of course, provide a relatively rational reconstruction of the events. One can point to the multiplicity of factors which affected each other in a "unique" way. One can bring the logic of the hellish event to light and to a certain extent clarify it.

94

But, confronted by the mountain of shoes that the victims left behind prior to the "disinfection," or the spectacles of every possible shape and size, or the suitcases and bags, large and small, this rational reconstruction proves not to be strong enough to dispel the strange mood and the sense of *the vanishing of the essential*. Whoever sees this has the feeling of standing over against something which has no essence, in the sense that it does not fit into any frame of reference.

The mystery does not coincide with the sorrow, the pain, the fear, and the humiliation of the victims. It is nourished by it and grows into an independent form which repeatedly withdraws from every fixed configuration. On the one hand, what we see before us in demonic and grotesque proportions is, in a certain regard, familiar. Whoever sees through the narcissistic illusion of self-glorification realizes how vulnerable one's own will is and how equivocal one's desire. On the other hand, the event remains alien for us. The mystery lies not only in the unimaginable proportions that evil took on in the Nazi death camps. It is also present in the smallest gesture in which human dignity becomes completely meaningless. The nonchalance and the taken for granted way this can occur is profoundly disorientating. The ease with which kapo Alex wipes his hand clean on a prisoner's shoulder in Primo Levi's *Is dit een mens* is a striking illustration of this.[4] As no other Primo Levi has portrayed, and precisely within the great story of the demonic happening of national socialism, the small betrayal that threatens us all.

The experience of being unable to speak does not imply that people fall silent. The awareness one is dealing with a dark mystery, accompanying being as a shadow, does not make evil and suffering absolutely meaningless. Questioning himself whether it is in fact meaningful to bear witness to the twilight life in the camp, Primo Levi writes: "I am convinced that not a single human experience is meaningless or to be neglected."[5]

But can one do *more* than bear witness, accuse, fight, in order to stave off forgetfulness with all possible means of expression? Can one also attain an understanding? Does the mystery of evil not withdraw from every attempt at *comprehension*? One could even ask whether it is in fact in good taste, or tact, to take indescribable suf-

fering up in a philosophical discourse and to want to clarify it rationally? Does thought not reach its limits here, in a much more fundamental manner than it was under discussion in Kant's critique? Is it
not a sign of wisdom to let oneself be inspired by the example of Job
and to give up the will to understand what is the most difficult for us
to bear—namely, the suffering of the innocent?

Sometimes it is no small temptation to say with Martin in
Voltaire's *Candide*: "Let us work without theorizing . . . it is the only
way to make life bearable."[6] And when the temptation arises to try to
provide a rational justification for everything, as is the case with
Pangloss in the same novel, then Candide, who has learned through
injury and shame to resist such attempts, utters his famous response: "Well said [Pangloss], but we must cultivate our garden."[7]

Voltaire's text is exceptionally well suited, with its ironic technique, to free us once and for all from the illusion of an unproblem-
atic rationalism. It cannot, however, satisfy when one chooses for a
more nuanced approach. Indeed, the problem of suffering and evil
only poses itself *as* a problem for those who try to understand. It is
only within the context and the project of a rational justification of
existence that it reveals its resistance, its recalcitrance. The will to
understand need not necessarily be identical to an attempt to disguise its gravity. It is only against the background of the question of
meaning that the threatening meaninglessness of evil really becomes manifest. Otherwise there is only a facticity about which one
can obtain knowledge, which is repulsive or that awakens horror,
but not a problem, and certainly not a mystery. Only for those who
chose for a responsible existence—and only the human being has
this possibility—does the challenge of suffering and evil arise. Our
own being compels us to a justification of what seems to withdraw
from every rational ground. "Living without theorizing" not only con-
tradicts what we are. It is perhaps not possible. Indeed, Martin's
statement in *Candide* functions as a sort of rationalization, as a position which is more than a mere fact, but which wants to pass for a
justified attitude toward an alleged problem.

From time immemorial the experience of evil and suffering has
given rise to the question how it can be harmonized with the exis-

tence of God. How can one affirm the existence of a being who as absolute perfection, as *omnitudo realitatis,* as moral creator, is called the ground of all actuality, when this actuality is completely permeated by all kinds of deficiencies, by suffering and evil?

The full scope of the problem appears when one does not limit oneself to the acceptance of an abstract and empty transcendence, but when one attributes to God the minimal intrinsic determination present in much of the Western tradition—namely, complete *goodness* and highest *power of being.* Without the latter, God would be reduced to a subjectively posited moral ideal and not understood as the ground of all that is. Without the former the absolute would coincide with actuality in its facticity. It would be a useless duplicate of all that is.[8] The problem arises in all its intensity when we have to do with *an actual ground thought of as absolute goodness.*

Here thought seems to contradict itself. It undergoes two fundamental experiences of thought within itself which, nonetheless, seem to exclude each other. Intellectual honesty bids us to hold on to both experiences and leave them in their truth as long as possible: *not to dispense with God on account of evil, and even less to obscure evil for the sake of God.*

We must go deeper and not let ourselves be tempted by the seduction of quick solutions which do not do sufficient justice to the actuality. Both kinds of experience of thought perhaps fecundate each other reciprocally. Perhaps we acquire a more adequate concept of God when we grant suffering and evil their full weight? Perhaps the mystery surrounding them will come to stand in a better perspective, when we see it in relation to the affirmation of God?

The Sting of Moral Evil—Before we attempt this, it is necessary to make some distinctions. We know intuitively that there is a fundamental difference between a natural disaster and an extermination camp, between bodily pain and humiliation, between dying and murder.

Thus we speak, on the one hand, of *physical evil* and mean thereby one or other lack a being might have from the viewpoint of its natural essence (for example, a bodily infirmity). *Moral evil,* on the other hand, refers to the will, to a conscious and free being. It is also a lack, a falling short of something—namely, of what is required from an ethical standpoint. From this initial description it appears that evil always refers to some *normative standard*. Without a normative conception of what is, one cannot speak of evil.[9] It always points to a falling short of, or being opposed to, what actually should be. Without this normative conception one can only speak about facts and patterns, or about the motives that determine their course. Correlatively, something is good, not only because it is, but because it is as it should be. In a derivative sense we sometimes speak of "success" and refer to the adequation between something and its normative form. In the way good refers to a correspondence between something and its concept, evil refers to a noncorrespondence, a lack, a falling short. That is why it is not possible to speak of *metaphysical evil* (or *absolute evil*) alongside physical and moral evil. In that case, it is no longer clear what the normative instance is to which the nonadequation or lack would apply. Then evil loses its relativity. It becomes something absolute, because outside the order of being nothing can be or be thought.[10] It would correspond with being as such—and then one cannot understand any more what enables us to call this being *bad*. In fact the *metaphysical pessimism* which originates with this idea usually comes down to a negative valuation of facticity in the name of something higher or better, something which is more true or which *is* more. Thus, here appears an ideality which itself no longer falls under the negative judgment. With this the idea of metaphysical evil meets its downfall, or in any case it is subject to contradiction.[11]

However, to speak of *physical evil* is also not as easy as it might appear at first sight. Is pain, as a signal of a bodily dysfunction, not to be called good? What would be evil in chemical processes which simply happen and cause volcanic eruptions and earthquakes? Is not this the logic proper to nature? Why connect the decay and death of living organisms with evil, when we know that their demise is inscribed in their very being? Why consider a genetic mutation which carries with it defects and shortcomings as something negative? Indeed, what could be the worth of a life consisting only of undisturbed fulfillment? Imagine there to be a technique that would immediately satisfy every desire the moment it occurred or which would fill every acute shortcoming, lack, or absence.[12] Every tension, and every tragedy would disappear from life. Such a thought-experiment evidently flirts with the notion of removing our *condition humaine*. But there is more. The aversion awakened by the thought which this experiment toys with is a sign that nonidentity, the absence of a pure and continuous coincidence in the here and now, is essential for our being. Desire is so essential that we—it sounds paradoxical—"can" never will the complete fulfillment of (our) desire. Such fulfillment is not just a phantasm, it also goes against the very dynamic of desire itself which leaves every fulfilment behind.

Perhaps we can only genuinely speak of physical evil in relation to the *human mode of being*. Only for the human being can sickness, suffering, and death be a problem. And this, precisely to the extent that the purely physical is transcended, to the extent that the human being is *more* than just a natural being. As a spiritual being, man suspends the immediate operation of nature and thus nature can become a problem. It is only in relation to a human project that the course of nature can be experienced as an obstacle. It is only for a will to live, to be healthy, to be at ease, to care for others, to communicate, to understand, and so on, that physical events are experienced as what ought not to be, what would be better otherwise, as what breaks down a relationship, leaves a project incomplete, hinders the care for others, obstructs thought, and so on.

Physical evil can only be spoken of *when the natural order is not adequate to the spiritual, human order*, when the order of nature collides with one's own existential project. *That is why* it is good to heal the sick, to defend human life with all the humane means at our disposal, to anticipate natural disasters as much as possible, and to relieve or remove pain and physical suffering wherever possible.

Physical evil is a sign of finitude, of the limitation of our freedom: never being wholly with ourselves in the other (nature).[13] To accept this inadequacy, while continuously trying to minimize it, that is, to accept the *condition humaine*, this is one of the most difficult tasks. The root of physical evil ultimately lies in ourselves in the inability to accept finitude. Through experience the human being can learn to recognize that the good is not identical with the pleasant.[14] Perhaps it is even more difficult to accept that the unpleasant is not equal to evil. What makes existence worthwhile and gives deeper contentment than every ephemeral pleasure is not situated at the level of our natural dimensions. It is to be found in the spiritual core of our whole being—namely, in the moral quality of the will. With this the person has a unique and irreplaceable value. It is also the place where the mystery of evil manifests its abysmal nature: the evil that we perpetrate against ourselves and others, a perversity that does not come from outside but hides in our most intimate and personal life.

This form of evil, moral evil (*das Böse* distinguished from *das Übel*), is the greatest challenge for any affirmation of God. The defect is here no longer relative to one's point of view (as with physical evil). It is absolute, because it consists in the denial of what is unconditionally valid, the moral law and its ground: the absolute value of the human person.

The place where evil shows itself in its hardest core is simultaneously the source of nourishment for all that is good. The moral core of the human being—by which the human being represents an absolute value, whatever other physical or spiritual qualities might there be—is also what motivates the fight against all the forms of evil connected with illness, pain, and every kind of physical and psychological suffering. This fight is a decisive form in which respect for the other is actively demonstrated.[15]

4.2 THE MYSTERY OF FREEDOM

Si malum est, Deus est (If evil exists, God exists). With this provocative sentence Thomas Aquinas responds to a question that Boethius utters through the mouth of a philosopher and that pithily formulates the entire problem of theodicy: *Si Deus est, unde malum?* (If God exists, whence comes evil?)[16] Thomas's argument for this remarkable reversal is clear and succinct. There would be no evil if there were no order of the good, the absence (privatio) of which is precisely evil. There would be no such order, if God did not exist. Here God and evil are mutually affirmed in the highest degree.

Nevertheless, despite the clarity of the position, the question remains: Whence this *privatio boni*? If God is the ground of everything, is God not also the ground of this deficiency? Why has God not placed humankind in existence in such a way that the human directed purely to the good? Does God perhaps will the perversity that hides in the human heart? Or, in case God does not will it, can God not prevent it? Nevertheless, in both cases it seems impossible to think evil together with God. Either God is not good, or God is powerless: in both cases not God.

Indeed, are such speculations not meaningless because they suggest that it is possible to speak from God's standpoint? Are they to be taken seriously, if one considers human history and all the evil and misery belonging to it?

The Refusal of Adorno—For many in contemporary philosophy, Auschwitz has become the sign, the unequivocal sign, of the evil that makes our history an unholy history.

For some humanity has here lost an illusion, definitively. It means the end of every justification of existence and also of God. Auschwitz is a *task*: henceforth to learn to live without theological illusions. It is the definitive end of every onto-theology.[17]

Adorno especially has shed light on this unholy history, of which Auschwitz is the apotheosis. For him Auschwitz is not an isolated fact. It is not an unfortunate incident in history. On the contrary, in all its horror it reveals the essence of history. The famous essay that Adorno wrote together with Horkheimer, *Dialectic of Enlightenment*, offers a sort of reversed Hegelian philosophy of history. History is not the process of progress in the consciousness of freedom. On the contrary, it is the process of increasing suppression, marginalization, and the eventual elimination of the individual. It is the realization of what is represented in the story of Odysseus and the Cyclops. In order to save himself from the violence of the Cyclops, Odysseus devises a ruse. When asked what his name is, Odysseus answers that his name is "nobody." Then when the Cyclops is drunk, his eye is gouged out by Odysseus. His cries for help, however, are ineffectual and are not taken seriously by the bystanders. Does the Cyclops, screaming from pain and anger, not exclaim it himself: *Nobody did it.*

In order to survive, Odysseus had to give up his individuality. He had to become "nobody."[18] The negation of the free individual represented in the story is essential for the history of the West. It is the result of a remarkable *dialectic of the Enlightenment* in which the process of emancipation turns into its opposite.

In this sense the Enlightenment has negated itself. The human being has tried to free itself from the power of nature. However, this endeavor has turned into its opposite. The emancipation by reason has led to an all-encompassing "reification." This manifests itself in a disturbed relation of humankind to nature, society, and himself.[19] Nature is degraded to mere material for technical intervention. It loses more and more of its reality. The control over nature leads to a complete desubstantializing. The power and the drive to control to which nature falls victim also has an effect on society. What was to become a "second free and spiritual actuality brought about by man himself" (Hegel), has become something in which the human being no longer recognizes itself. Society has become a repressive system. The means of controlling the violence of nature has become an independent power against humanity. The dependence on nature is now replaced by the oppression by reason. The reification of nature is, as it were, internalized. It has affected the essence of the human being and society itself and has placed everything under the regime of *externality*.

Adorno sees many ways in which this downfall of the Enlightenment is realized in contemporary culture. In *Capitalism* in which the human becomes a slave to a commodity fetishism. In the *Sciences* and the corresponding domination of a formal, quantitative rationality, in which the individual is reduced to a statistical factor. In modern *politics of art and culture* which has deteriorated to an amusement industry and whose commercialization and standardization suppress all individuality and creativity. In *politics* where particular interests dominate over universality and solidarity. And preeminently, and with all clarity, in *fascism*: there the free individual no longer counts. In all this is visible the degeneration of reason. It is reduced to a power which identifies everything, equalizes: "To think is to identify,"[20] which means cataloguing, fixing, depriving something of its proper essence. That is why it must be said against Hegel: *Das Ganze ist das Unwahre.*[21] Of this Auschwitz is the definitive seal.

Auschwitz has changed everything. Since Auschwitz everything must be thought anew. "All post-Auschwitz culture, including its urgent critique, is garbage."[22] This refers to the "grand words" that philosophy has uttered in metaphysics: "After Auschwitz there is no word tinged from on high, not even a theological one, that has any right unless it undergoes a transformation."[23]

In his work Adorno bears witness to this necessary transformation. The classic metaphysical conceptions of God and the immortality of the soul are changed into utopian signs. They express the negation of this (bad) actuality and refer to an other (more) genuine possibility. They represent the hope in an "other," in a new, successful relationship between humankind and nature and among human beings.[24] Thinking about God does not mean a conceptual understanding of the highest being. It has a different function. It manifests the possibility of countering the despair to which history and its culmination in Auschwitz exposes us. It is no longer theoretically relevant. It is completely reduced to an expression of the will not to resign oneself to (the) existing reality. After Auschwitz one cannot continue with metaphysics. Its condition of possibility, the all-identifying reason, was after all also the condition of possibility *of* Auschwitz. Yet plain silence is also impossible, because that would indirectly be the definitive affirmation of Auschwitz. Every perspective on transcendence would then be closed.[25] The new "metaphysics" can therefore only appear in the form of negativity.

It has repeatedly been pointed out that Adorno's thought runs aground on unsolvable aporias.[26] Indeed, Adorno is very much aware of the perilous nature of his entire endeavor. Philosophy appears to be an attempt to bring to expression that which withdraws from every expression. In its negative dialectic it remains bound to the categories of the philosophy of identity which it nonetheless wants to break.[27]

Whether Adorno's philosophical project is thus doomed to fail, whether it is an impossible project, I now leave aside. It is however the case that the *utopian negation of the perverse world does not make the mystery of evil any less enigmatic.* The practical-utopian negation sets itself against every attempt to understand evil theoretically. This last would amount to the acceptance of evil. Evil remains as an absolute recalcitrant reality. But the question remains whether it could show itself *as evil* without the utopian perspective. Adorno, of course, is not Thomas Aquinas who makes God, in a paradoxical way, into a "condition of the possibility" of evil (*Si malum est, Deus est*). In Adorno there is no metaphysical order in relation to which evil appears as a *privation.* However, if evil were absolute, then it could not appear as such, as has been argued above. Adorno's thought cannot evade this dialectical necessity. However incomprehensible it might be, evil is accompanied by this minimal intelligibility.

Whosoever tries to think about (moral) evil must simultaneously consider something like a nonillusory good actuality, even if it can—according to Adorno's logic—hardly be described in a positive manner.

Kant: Evil and Freedom—Can one go even further? Can one affirm simultaneously God as the ground of all that is, as "good power of being," and evil, without taking the sting out of evil? Can one understand evil in one way or another without reducing it? On this question Kant has gone to the outmost extreme. He connects the mystery of evil with another mystery, that of freedom. Whether thus, via a detour, evil is placed in God, we will discuss in the following section. Our attention is now primarily directed at the connection Kant works out between evil and freedom.

"That in the world evil has its way, is a complaint as old as history." With this Kant begins the first part of his text on the philosophy of religion: *Religion within the Limits of Reason Alone*(1793).[28] It is reminiscent of a famous Hegelian expression that the history of the world is as a "slaughter bench" and that "the periods of happiness in it are the blank pages."[29]

Such pessimism, or better, realism, among other things, already played a role years earlier in Kant's book: *Idea for a Universal History from a Cosmopolitan Point of View* (1784). In this text the question of the possiblity of what is given to humankind as its highest task—namely, the realization of a society governed by the principle of right (a universal civic society which administers law among humans)—leads to a great problem.[30] In the famous *Sixth Thesis* Kant states that such an order, in addition to other considerations, also presupposes the activity of a good will. How can this be guaranteed by a being who obviously does not have a holy will—"[who] will always abuse his freedom." Or even: "The human is an animal who, if it lives among others of its kind, requires a master."[31]

In his small occasional text on the philosophy of history, Kant speculates further about how such an order of right becomes possible, from which powers one can expect the realization of a society guided by the principle of right. On the other hand, in the first part of his text on the philosophy of religion, he as it were plunges into the depths and reflects on the origin of evil. In this journey to the depths Kant will discover a mysterious perversity of the human will. Thus he goes against the optimistic conceptions of the Enlightenment.[32] Some were surprised to read such things in Kant.[33] In an ironical manner, on June 7, 1793, Goethe wrote to Herder: "After a long life of purifying his philosophical cloak of all sorts of prejudices that besmirched it, Kant has now shamefully stained it with radical evil, so that Christians also would be tempted to kiss its hem."[34]

Kant's doctrine of evil does not pay lip service in any way to his Christian readers. It is not a flaw but an essential part of his answer to the question of questions: *What is man?*[35] In virtually all of Kant's works lie clues to the theory that is only explicitly developed in *Die Religion*.

Kant's vision differs radically from the prevailing rationalistic theodicy of Leibniz and his followers.[36] His criticism is that such a theodicy does not reach its goal. Instead of justifying God, it compromises God and humankind. It does not preserve God's goodness and it does an injustice to humankind. This is evident in the core of the argument which again and again returns in different forms. The first idea is: God does not want suffering and evil, but he cannot prevent them, since they follow from human finitude. The second thought is: from the perspective of infinitude, evil and suffering is sublated in the encompassing process of world harmony as a developmental factor, as an instrument in the realization of perfection. This theory must, however, overshoot its target. *A god is justified, but it is a God other than the one originally intended.* In any case, God is no longer the absolute perfection who unites goodness and the power of being in oneself. An injustice is also done to humankind. By placing evil within finitude itself, the human being is deprived of its freedom and responsibility.

We thus arrive at one of the most essential points of Kant's theory.

The ground of evil lies *in the human person and human freedom*. The problem is thus restricted to *moral evil*, that which we do onto ourselves and others, something for which we bear responsibility. What about the earthquake in Lisbon which for many in the eighteenth century was the shock that unsettled their rationalistic optimism: Is it perhaps not evil? And what of all the other kinds of natural disasters, all the diseases, suffering, death, all the injustice that befalls us?

In the first place, what counts is the great *theoretical restriction* which characterizes Kant's thought. Despite all his sympathy for physico-theology, the world of nature remains for the most part a closed book. God's creation is not transparent. Theoretical insight into the highest goal of everything, into the ultimate meaning of all that happens, is not possible. There is no experience that could be the basis of such a knowing.

In addition to this theoretical restriction there is the primacy of *practical reason*. From a practical point of view, that is, with a view to the realization of a good will, something can be said about evil, insofar as it is something which befalls us and exceeds our freedom, evil as *Übel* (as distinguished from what corresponds to our freedom, moral evil, the *Böse*).

The evil that strikes us in so many ways, teaches us that *happiness* is not our highest destiny (happiness understood as the highest and most enduring fulfillment of our desires). So, for example, the Lisbon earthquake shows us that it could not be our destiny to build "eternal huts" on the stage of finitude.

Considered metaphysically, it does not follow that finitude is bad. God's creation is good. The concept of God necessitates absolutely holding on to this. Evil must not be ontologized. Nor does Manichaeism follow from this. The ultimate meaning of all that happens cannot be made transparent theoretically. What can be drawn from it is a *practical* lesson. Lisbon affirms what we already knew from moral experience: *what is highest for the human being is not happiness, but the worthiness of happiness.* There is a dimension that exceeds all natural fulfillment.

The sting of the affirmation of God lies in *moral evil.* How is this to be understood?

To answer this question it is important to bring it before the mind as clearly as possible. What does Kant mean by moral evil? Obviously evil bound up with human free will. This is, however, still too vague, too general. Moral evil is more specific. According to Kant it lies in the *intention*, in the orientation of the will. It lies in the maxims, the subjective principles that guide actions. It does not lie in the effect of actions, but in the intention that inspires the action. That intention is morally bad which places individual particularity above the universal command of the moral law. In other words, evil lies in the will to be an exception, while the rule holds for others.[37] Formulated more concretely: moral evil lies in not recognizing the humanity in myself and others as an end in itself, in the instrumentalization of what makes the human being a person. What is the ground of this?

Kant calls the ground, that which lies at the root of all particular bad moral actions, *radical evil.* At stake here is a fundamental perversion of striving and willing. The word *radical* means exactly what it says: that which lies at the root (*radix*) of everything. It is fundamentally distinguished from *absolute.* This fundamental distinction is legitimized by something of which we have seen that it can in no way be doubted: the *fact of reason (Faktum der Vernunft).* This shows that the human being is aware of standing under the absolute command of the moral law. If radical evil were to be understood as something absolute, then this openness to the moral imperative would be impossible. Were the human being completely corrupt, there would be no *Faktum*, and the imperative *could* not be obeyed. Without a minimal openness to the good, the imperative would be reduced to something meaningless. "Radical" thus is fundamentally different from "absolute." The human being is not a diabolical being. It has an original *predisposition* toward the *good*.[38] This predisposition consists of the receptivity of a certain feeling: a *respect* for the moral law as a sufficient motive for the will. This openness for the good is *original*, which means that it "is bound up with the possibility of human nature." Without this openness the human being would not be a human being. That is why Kant speaks of a *predisposition* (*Anlage*): "By the predisposition of a being we understand not only its constituent elements which are necessary to it, but also the forms of their combination, by which the being is what it is."[39]

This openness for the good is broken by a *propensity to evil*: radical evil, that lies at the root of all particular evil. What is at issue here is the tendency to make the natural inclinations into the last determining ground of the will, thus turning the moral order on its head.[40] This propensity can take different forms. So there is what Kant calls "the *frailty* (*fragilitas*) of human nature": a sort of weakness in a person's ability to consistently follow the moral law, which he has made into a guiding principle of his maxims, when it conflicts with particular inclinations. So there is the "*impurity* (*impuritas*) of the human heart," which means that the moral law does not suffice as the only motive, but that it is only active when combined with other, nonmoral motives. Finally, there is the malignity in which the moral order is reversed. It is the "*perversity* of the human heart": the inclination to make wrong maxims the determining ground of the will.[41]

However, moral evil is not in any way explained by this. Indeed, the question that now arises is: Whence this propensity to evil, this perversity of the heart?

To be able genuinely to appreciate Kant's answer to this question, one point is of central importance. Kant does not speak of a *pre-*

disposition (Anlage), but of *the propensity to evil (Hang zum Bosen)*. He defines "propensity" as follows: "By *propensity (propensio)* I understand the subjective ground of the possibility of an inclination (habitual craving, *concupiscentia*) so far as humankind in general *is liable to it*. A propensity is distinguished from a predisposition by the fact that although it can indeed be innate, it *ought* not to be represented merely thus; for it can also be regarded as having been *acquired* (if it is good), or *brought* by humankind *upon itself* (if it is evil)."[42]

Propensity points to something belonging to human nature that must be conceived, at the same time, as *brought* by humankind *upon* itself *(zugezogen)*. This something must *also* be the work of freedom. It is something for which humankind is responsible. Radical evil belongs to our *condition humaine* while yet being something contingent. Where it not in part contingent, it would weigh on us as a natural necessity. It would make it impossible to comply with the "you ought" of the moral law. The moral law would become a meaningless command, and this cannot be the case within Kant's conception of reality.[43]

Radical evil is a corruption that arises within a being which is good by nature. The predisposition toward good is therefore primary. The fundamental structure of the human being, namely, reason— cannot be bad. Kant thus claims that the human being as such is created good.[44] Yet, the human good is not actualized by this. That only happens when the human being incorporates the good motives, contained in human predisposition, in maxims. If humans do not do so, they bring evil upon themselves. There is a fundamental relation with freedom. It is because of this that Kant rejects those theories that situate the origin of evil in the *animal* nature of the human being, or in society. Kant also rejects the idea of *original sin*, understood as a biologically inherited *corruption*.[45] Radical evil can only be moral if it concerns something toward which man has freely adopted an attitude. It is inextricably bound up with *freedom*. It is something that belongs to us. It follows from this that it is *impossible to explain its origin*. Kant writes: *"there is then for us no conceivable ground from which the moral evil in us could originally have come."*[46]

If freedom could be *explained*, that is, traced back to one cause or other, this explanation would immediately neutralize freedom. It would no longer be *self*-determination but would be determined by something else. The issue of moral evil is an analogous problematic. Were it a sort of ontological defect or completely caused from outside, the human being could not be held responsible. Evil would lose its moral significance. There is no solution as to why we are susceptible to the temptation to reverse the moral order and to make our natural inclinations the decisive determining ground of our actions. Like freedom it is without explanation.

Kant characterizes evil not just as *privatio boni*. He traces it back to an essential quality of the will (malignity, but not diabolical malignity). Yet for him evil is also something secondary. It is *perversio*: a reversal of the moral order, secondary with respect to the original orientation toward the good. In this sense it points to a *lack*, because it signifies the absence of the right order in which things *essentially* should be.[47] Because of its connection with freedom, evil remains, for Kant, shrouded in an impenetrable mystery. Nevertheless this mystery is not absolute, because moral evil springs forth from the human. It has its root in the *will*.[48]

This impenetrability seems to be the price that must be paid for an unreserved acceptance of the human being as a moral and responsible being. And this was apodictically evident for Kant.

We are, then, not dealing here with a morbid orientation to sin. This seems so only for a culture which has outgrown feelings of guilt by situating guilt always elsewhere (society, history, the family, parents, psychic life, bodily constitution). Kant's doctrine of radical evil is the obverse side of his *theory of freedom*. There is no place for such a doctrine when people have reduced education and formation to a refined form of conditioning. With Kant's theory our inquiry does not come to an end. If thought can undergo the experience of having to affirm God, how can God be understood as the ground of a being whose will is so susceptible to the *perversity* of evil?

Thought must return to the experiences which lead to these affirmations.

4.3 THE ROSE AND THE CROSS

God and Evil—Having faced evil, thinking must return to and reflect upon its previous experiences. If it wants to be coherent with itself, it cannot leave the affirmation of God and the reality of evil juxtaposed and unrelated. One thing is certain: because of authentic experiences of thought, it knows itself as bound to both sides.

A link will only succeed subsequent to the deepening of both affirmations. Perhaps one thought can fecundate the other and vice versa. Thought must not take the short, easy way by eliminating *one* of the two terms: God because of evil, or the recalcitrance of evil for the sake of God. It would cease to be faithful to the experiences of thought it had undergone. It would mutilate itself. So it must chose a detour, the way of deepening. In so doing it will experience new things about itself and actuality.

The first thing to which this confrontation between God and evil leads is the necessity of a renewed emphasis on God's transcendence. God cannot function as a kind of explanatory factor in scientific argumentation. Kant's critique of the proofs of God's existence (in the limited hermeneutics given by Kant to these proofs) has comprehensively brought this to light. This means that God is not the "cause" of something, for instance evil, as warmth is the cause of the expansion of iron. God is not to be understood as a worldly cause that might replace natural causation or the causality of freedom. It perhaps sounds paradoxical, but a God who would make evil impossible would for us perhaps be less "bearable" than a God who does not "prevent" it. After all, as a sort of great worldly being, such a God would deprive the other beings of their space to be themselves.

A large part of modern atheism is grounded in such a conception of God. Consider, for example, Sartre.[49] In the light of such an absolute, human freedom would evaporate. The human being would find itself faced with the alternative of choosing for itself and rejecting God, or vice versa. It strikes a chord with us when someone says that after Auschwitz God can no longer be contemplated. Given humanity's experience of suffering and all the evil accompanying our history, it would be seductive if one could claim that what is needed is an "other" concept of God, in which God is a powerless God, who suffers from our suffering.

But are not such ideas grounded in the fact that one does not fully adhere to God's transcendence? If we think of God as a being that has a future, that waits on our actions, that is powerless in our history of suffering, do we not introduce all sorts of anthropomorphism? Does God not become a "being" among beings?[50]

Against this it must be argued that in the experiences of thought that have been developed as ways to God, the *qualitative* difference between God and finite beings is an essential element. God is "other." God is the *absolute*. Face to face with evil we must maintain this, without any hesitation, as we must also do when confronted by the reality of freedom. God becomes merely an impossible competitor for our freedom, or someone who must be expelled due to the reality of evil, if we have first weakened God's transcendence, or if we imagine God as a being guilty of Nazi camps, or that he cannot prevent them, or threatens our freedom or even makes a show of it (everything is already decided!). For in all these considerations God is involved in an intraworldly causality, even though this can be veiled in a sophisticated way.

The experience of evil does not lead to the elimination of the Absolute, but to the necessity, free from every anthropomorphism, to maintain its transcendence.

When we go this way, however, we encounter new problems. Is not something just as essential to the concept of God denied— namely, that God is understood as the transcendent *ground* of everything? I think we must be consistent here. *God is the ground of everything*, thus also of a freedom for which evil is a possibility and a reality. God does not cause what that freedom does, but makes it to be as such. Otherwise God would not be the Absolute, but limited by something "else," by something that is no longer relative to divinity.

All this barely solves anything. Here thought clearly reaches its limits. We are inclined to question further. How can God be the ground of a being that in its freedom can go against its own being? How is this to be reconciled with God's perfection, God's essential goodness? Can God not bring a better freedom into being? Here we must adhere to the elementary requirement of coherence. What do we think at all if we speak of a *freedom* that would *necessarily* chose the good? Does this not come down to a refusal to accept freedom as such?

What is essential for free acts indeed is that they are solely grounded in themselves. To explain them by tracing them back to something else would signify denying them. The "choice" of the free will for evil confronts us with something unfathomable, in the sense that it cannot be traced back to anything further. *In this sense God is not the ground of evil*. It has its mysterious root in the essence of freedom. A freedom in which the possibility for evil would not be present, would not be a better freedom. *It simply would not be freedom*.

Of course, our freedom is not absolute. That is why a reflection on evil, in which the link with freedom is central, has its limitations. Besides the *ethical* approach to evil followed thus far, there is also a *tragic* approach.[51] In that approach the finitude of freedom stands in the foreground. Free action is not pure creation. It is *liberté-en-situation*, not absolute originality.

Freedom finds itself in a history that is partially an unholy history. We choose and act in a world that has always already been affected by evil, one that provokes evil. This tragic moment is also expressed in the symbolism of the *original sin*: although Adam chooses freely, the snake who manipulates the fall through its lies is already present *prior* to Adam's decision. The story expresses in symbolic terms what is a general human experience—namely, that evil in part befalls us, that in one way or other it infects or drags us along with it.

The givenness of freedom and the affirmation of God constrain us from making this tragic dimension into a cosmic or ontological reality. In the same way as it came to the fore in the symbolism of the original sin, evil resides in the human heart. For the human being is *seduced* and not necessitated.

Put otherwise: "the power of evil is not beyond freedom."[52] Reflection on God and evil leads to a deepening of the reality of both. It leads to a renewed affirmation of God's transcendence and to an emphasis on the ethical dimension of evil. More than before it sheds light on the mysterious manner in which God is the ground of everything, the ground on which the human body exists as a free being. But, and this is probably the most important result, it makes us aware of the *limits* of thought. It is indeed remarkable that not a single solution to the problem of evil that has been devised in the history of Western thought is truly satisfactory. The recalcitrance of evil lies in its strange ontological status. This has been described in the previous paragraphs. Evil can only be understood in negative terms: wrongness, destruction, perversion, denial. In all its horror it is something parasitic, something secondary. Its horribleness only becomes apparent against the background of a fundamental orientation toward the good. It is dark, because we stand out toward the light.

Plotinus has expressed this in a striking manner.[53] Plotinus compares the difficulty of understanding evil with the peculiarity of seeing the darkness. In order to see darkness, the light must withdraw, otherwise darkness cannot set in. But how to see something when there is no light? In the light I cannot see the darkness due to the light. But in darkness I cannot see the darkness, because there is no light. There is but *one* possibility of seeing darkness—namely, not seeing anything; that is, not to see. The seeing of darkness consists in not seeing.

Somewhat in line with Kant, perhaps we must seek the ultimate meaning of trying to think God and evil together more in its practical relevance than in the speculative result. By this we mean the following.

Evil is Not Absolute—By opposing God to evil, it loses some of its weight, despite the terrible forms it can assume. *It turns out not be something absolute.* This thought can be the ground of hope, rooted in the faith that the perversion of actuality is not its truth. By situating evil in the human will, in the perversity of the human heart, we break the bewitchment that can emanate from a fatalistic interpretation. This understanding is also an invitation to connect evil with our responsibility and to seek to do good.

Perhaps it sounds paradoxical, but the idea that the mystery of evil is rooted in the mystery of freedom, is perhaps *the most human solution*: it does not relieve us of our responsibility and does not rob us of our freedom. It is perhaps also the most *divine solution* because it is in harmony with the essence of the Absolute as it manifests itself in the experiences of thought: mysterious immanence of a radical transcendence. God *and* freedom: affirming them together is especially difficult because people frequently consider relationships *privative*, in this sense that what the one does, the other does not. If we seek for an *analogy* (one cannot go much further), then the most obvious causality is the one typical of love. Here what one does is not a limitation for the other. Quite the contrary, the more *determined* by the other, the more the self can be *itself*. It sounds paradoxical: the more God encompasses us, the more free we are. However, as already stated, this is no more than an analogy. God's causality cannot be compared in any way to a worldly causality. Evil is thus not thought away. What is excluded is the interpretation in which evil withdraws from *every* concept and becomes something absolute.

Philosophy cannot be anything more than, as Hegel put it, the rose *(die Rose)* in the cross of the present *(Kreuz der Gegenwart)*. It can reveal that reason is not absent in this actuality, without thereby legitimizing everything. Indeed, the *present* also remains in the sign of the cross.

Here philosophy is consolation and reconciliation with what is— *de consolatione philosophiae*. It does not do this by calling everything good, but by arguing that *in the end no truth belongs to evil*. Evil must be understood as the *failure* of the good toward which humans are essentially orientated. It is not be identified with the *essential ground* of actuality.

This is not a pious sigh. For *why* is evil such a problem, why does it oppress us, why do we repudiate it? Finally only because we are certain of something. This something is very difficult to reconcile with the experience of evil—namely, that the good is the destiny and the deepest essence of the human being. In other words: it is because God is the ground of all that is, that evil is a parasitic perversion of the good, an obstacle for and a limit of thought.

115

Si malum est, Deus est. In light of these considerations Thomas's judgment appears to receive its full weight. Obviously, this judgment loses all meaning for those who have given up every order and for whom good and evil continually turn into each other. In the cynicism that speaks in this view, not only does the good become *semblance*, evil also loses its sting. In the end philosophy disappears because the idea of truth is abandoned.

5
Human Finitude and the Presence of God

It seems possible to take one's distance from the logic of what dominates: the absence of the essential. No one is the source of all he or she thinks. We are not gods but mortals. Yet we are not condemned merely to repeat the dominant form of life or *Weltanschauung*. Thought reveals the freedom needful to become conscious of what dominates and sometimes bewitches us. It allows for the establishment of a minimum distance in which the seductive effect of various *idols* is critically breached. This is apparent in part from the ability to *undergo experiences* in which our view of ourselves and actuality is altered. Thinking is not condemned to the here and now. On the contrary, the here and now is only accessible because thought in itself always already proceeds much further relative to the totality. Thinking can have the experience that what seems impossible must be kept open as a real possibility. It can acquire the experience that it and its world is other than what it *meant*.

It can develop other experiences of thought, the experiences of thought of others. It is invited to this by the desire for truth, the ideal of strict and coherent thought, and the will to radical intellectual honesty.

This can be a conclusion of the ways we have investigated thus far. They are not ways along which God's existence has been proved, in the manner it has been proven that the earth turns around the sun and not the other way around. Indeed, God is not a "being" in the way that natural and cultural objects are. God is not an object about which decisions can be made in a separate reflection. As the ground of all that is, origin and telos of all actuality, God is not external to what we ourselves are. As Augustine says, God is "more inward than my deepest innerness."[1]

117

The ways we have been tried have revealed experiences that thinking can go through when it attempts to understand the enigmatic contingency of existence. Or when it asks itself how wide its reach is, and what it means to think the absolute. Or what the conditions of possibility of the ethical are. With the term experience, frequently used in this context, I have wanted to indicate the processive, the *dialectical* element, yes, the adventure of philosophical thought. Moreover, "experience" is especially suitable for pointing out the *objective reference* of what is thought, to emphasize that it is not just a subjective construction. Experience is also often referred to in order to unmask alleged knowledge or to bring down problematic theoretical structures.[2] In the foregoing, this objective reference proved to be a constant. The affirmation of God resulted from the realization of not being able to do otherwise, of being confronted with a kind of necessity outside our own power, or of being submitted to a logic that, as it were, befalls one's subjective understanding. The affirmation referred to something *actual* that, though in no way open to experience in any sensuous manner, is actuality as such.

I have spoken of experiences that thinking *can* go through. It does not necessarily go through them. Many do not go the way we have gone thus far. Thought goes all sorts of ways, often ways that in no respect bring it into contact with something absolute. Though fundamentally directed toward universality, philosophical thought turns out to be permeated by particularity. This does not detract from the fact that what is thought has a *reference to truth*.

Something is intended that must in principle be valid for everyone who wants to think. Because of this remarkable connection between universal and particular, to which I will return, philosophical standpoints remain in principle subject to discussion. They have a certain provisional character. To a degree, they are *proposals* for purposes of explaining what is.[3] In the proposal I have worked out, it became clear that neither Kant's theoretical critique, nor the practical critique from the experience of suffering and evil, definitively close off ways of thought to God. Rather it was shown that these forms of critique have a purifying effect. And also that thought truly reaches the utmost limits of its possibilities.

In this last chapter I examine yet another challenge to the thinking of God. This is perhaps the most fundamental challenge. It has notably been expressed in the work of Heidegger and Nietzsche. It consists in a radicalizing of the *finitude* of our existence.[4] It is such a radicalization that thought is no longer able to move beyond the limits of finitude. Here all ground seems to fall away from every form of thinking about God, because the condition of possibility of such thinking is no longer present.

Does intellectual honesty not necessitate accepting that the ways toward God are no more than *historical forms* of thought that are dependent upon a specific understanding of Being? Moreover, must it not *now* be fully accepted, by a thought that has matured and in all lucidity confronts finitude, that an affirmation of the Absolute is no longer possible? From this point of view thought receives a new task: to accept the *nothingness* that surrounds every existence and every value. Instead of mourning the *loss* of the Absolute, precisely this loss must be appreciated as *gain*. Finitude is then no longer thought metaphysically in relation to the infinite, but as a positive reality in itself. The disappearance of metaphysical discourse about God is then the *freeing* of finitude.

In what follows we look more deeply into this problematic of finitude. I ask myself what its significance can be for a philosophical affirmation of God. It is clear that my interpretation here is *parti pris*. The *positive* moment yielded by our reflection hitherto on God is not abandoned. I also try to some extent to take stock of the preceding chapters. Here the theme of *God's presence* assumes a central position. This concluding chapter is then a kind of response to the opening chapter in which the theme of *absence* prevailed.

It will be shown that the presence of the essential—of God— can only be understood when thought, in Hegel's words, abandons all tenderness for the finite—that is to say, when finitude is truly recognized as finite, and not in a concealed way made into something absolute. The question is whether this *Aufhebung* of the finite can be made philosophically plausible. This is a question that, inspired by Hegel, I develop in discussion with Heidegger and Nietzsche.

5.1 FINITUDE AS BOUNDARY

Heidegger: The Desacralisation of the World—In his *Letter on Humanism* (1947) Martin Heidegger sets himself against those who consider his philosophy a form of atheism.[5] This interpretation is not just hasty; it is simply false. Heidegger refers in this context to earlier texts in which the point is evident. Thus he writes in *The Essence of Reasons* (1929): by the ontological interpretation of *Dasein* as Being-in-the-world, neither a positive nor negative judgment is made about any being toward the God of humankind.[6] But he goes on to say that this too can be misunderstood. In that case, the "deferral" at play here appears as a kind of apathy toward the question of religion, an indifference that falls victim to nihilism.

Heidegger's position is neither atheistic nor agnostic. It has a character entirely unto itself: *our thought about God comes too early.* What we try to do is premature. If we ask about God, we hardly know what we are inquiring about because we no longer know what "being" means. Or because we have lost the sense of the mystery of being and unconsciously identify "being" with a certain sense of being—namely, the objectivity of being-at-hand. Due to this dominant understanding of being, our thinking about God runs aground, must run aground, and loses its significance for the human being. Such thinking is for Heidegger characteristic of the whole of Western metaphysics: God conceived as the highest being which is the ultimate explanation of all that is. That such a thinking runs aground is demonstrated by the outcome of the history of Western metaphysics. This outcome is philosophically completed in the thought of *Nietzsche* and on a more general cultural level in the planetary domination of *technology*.

At first sight this can seem strange. However, for Heidegger there is a deep affinity between these two. This affinity lies in their *nihilistic* character. All actuality and truth become a function in a process that is completely without ground. Everything that is is reduced to material for a making that lacks any goal and norm other than its own praxis. I will come back to this.

Heidegger's problematization of a philosophical concept of God is of a very special nature. As appears from the *Letter on Humanism*,

God cannot be adequately thought. The reasons for this are not of an epistemological nature, as they are in Kant. The problem also does not lie in the existential protest that suffering and evil can evoke. No, if thought does not succeed in thinking God, this is because it is imprisoned in the framework of metaphysics. This results in what Nietzsche will openly pronounce: God is dead.

To come into proximity with a thinking about God many other, decisive things must happen. Heidegger writes: "Only from the truth of Being can the essence of the holy be thought. Only from the essence of the holy is the essence of the 'divinity' (*von Gottheit*) thought. Only in the light of the essence of divinity can it be thought or said what the word 'God' is to signify (*nennen soll*)."[7] The question of God can only be developed when the human being again gains access to the dimension to which the question belongs—namely, the dimension of the holy. Without a "sense" of the holy, the question of God is not adequately posed.

Now it is perhaps the case, according to Heidegger, that the peculiarity of contemporary world history lies in the fact that the dimension of the holy is blocked off (*Verschlossenheit*): "perhaps that is the sole malignancy (*Unheil*)."[8] This inaccessibility is rooted in something more profound, in the mystery of Being itself. The dimension of the holy remains blocked "if the open region of Being is not lighted and in its lighting is near man."[9] This proximity does not come about in traditional metaphysics. The God that is thought in traditional metaphysics is the God of the philosophers: *causa sui*, ground and cause, the ultimate explanation of all that is, is "ultimately a very ungodly god."[10]

In *Identity and Difference* Heidegger writes that godless thinking, that is, the thinking that abandons the God of philosophy (God as *causa sui*), is perhaps closer to God. It is "more open to Him."[11] Heidegger's views here are not without ambiguities.

On the one hand, he seems to take up a reformation, Barthian position, thus creating an unbridgeable chasm between faith and thinking, theology and philosophy. The "God of the philosophers" is then something completely different from the "God of faith." The certainty of faith and the "questionable character"(*Fraglichkeit*) of thought are two domains separated from each other by an abyss.[12] To the God of philosophy, as it is said in *Identity and Difference*, the human being can neither pray nor sacrifice. Before God as *causa sui*, human beings cannot fall to their knees in awe, nor can they play music and dance for such a God.

On the other hand, something more fundamental than the prevailing opposition between the "God of Pascal" and the "God of philosophy" seems to be at stake. The entire religious experience has become extremely problematic. It is itself pulled along into a darkening of being to which metaphysical thought explicitly bears witness. *Every* basis for thinking about God seems to have been lost with this. In *What are Poets for?* Heidegger writes that our history reveals something very decisive. We live in an age of godlessness. "Not only have the gods fled, but the divine radiance has become extinguished in world history."[13] And in *The Age of the World Picture* the loss of the gods (*Entgötterung*) is referred to as the fifth decisive characteristic of modernity. This is not the same as what is usually called secularization. Heidegger has something very specific in mind with this term. He writes the following:

> This expression does not mean the mere doing away with the gods, gross atheism. The dedivinization is a twofold process. On the one hand, the world picture is Christianized inasmuch as the cause of the world is posited as infinite, unconditional, absolute. On the other hand, Christendom transforms Christian doctrine into a *Weltanschauung* (the Christian *Weltanschauung*), and in that way makes itself modern and up to date. The loss of the gods is the situation of indecision regarding God and the gods. Christendom has the greatest share in bringing it about. But the loss of the gods is so far from excluding religiosity that rather only through that loss is the relation to the gods changed into mere "religious experience." When this occurs, the gods have fled. The resultant void is compensated for by means of historiographical and psychological investigation of myth."[14]

In any case, this difficult-to-interpret text shows that the phenomenon of the loss of the gods surpasses the prevailing opposition between belief and unbelief (here in the form of Christian faith and atheism).[15] What is at stake is a more profound event that encompasses the contemporary forms of belief and unbelief. The loss of the gods cannot be understood in terms of atheism. On the contrary, atheism must be understood as the expression of something deeper. It must be thought from the standpoint of the loss of the gods. That this loss and atheism are not to be identified with each other is already apparent from the fact that the loss of the gods is not equal to the decline of Christianity in modern culture. Rather it is connected to the emergence of a well-defined form of religiosity that Heidegger calls "religious experience" (*Das religiöse Erleben*). This will be explained below.

Heidegger, in the cited passages, does not give an explanation of that deeper event. Its *essential origin* remains in the dark. He does however characterize its various aspects and points to the large role that Christianity played in its ascendancy (*Heraufführung*).

It is an event that has two sides. On the one hand, it concerns a Christianization of the image of the world. We see this taking place in the great metaphysical systems of modernity, in which the ultimate ground of actuality is interpreted in light of the God of the Bible. The ground of the world is understood as the infinite, as the unconditional, or the absolute. Heidegger here refers, perhaps implicitly, to Descartes, Kant, and Hegel respectively. The loss of the divine shows itself in the onto-theological structure of metaphysics. It is connected with the nihilism that is essential to the metaphysics in which Being is understood as a highest being. Although the God of the philosophers is interpreted in the light of the Christian religion, that can only happen—God can only enter philosophy—by virtue of the nature of metaphysics *itself*, on the basis of its essentially onto-theological structure.[16] This Christianization of the world in the great metaphysical systems of modernity implies a dedivinization. This is not primarily due to Christendom as such, but rather to the structure of metaphysics in which it is inscribed. Here Heidegger points to the internal kinship between the God of Christian theology and metaphysics that he develops further elsewhere.

It is well known that Christian theology has assimilated quite a few elements from Greek philosophy. However, it is not the case that

God first enters philosophy through Christian theology. According to Heidegger, God was always already present in philosophy by virtue of the nature of metaphysics. That is why Greek philosophy could be taken up by Christian theology. The deepest roots of the loss of the divine lie in the essence of metaphysics itself.

This Christianization of the world is at the same time a secularization of Christianity. This is the *other side* of the loss of the gods: a degradation of the Christian faith into a worldview. Faith thereby surrenders what is authentic to it and assimilates itself to the spirit of modernity (it reinterprets its Christianity as a *Weltanschauung*). It loses its essence in order to win its modernity. The distinction at play here is elucidated elsewhere. Heidegger makes an essential distinction between *Christendom* and *Christianity*: "Christendom . . . and the Christianity of the New Testament faith are not the same."[17] By Christendom Heidegger understands the historical, worldly-political appearance of the church with its social power and its decisive role within the shaping of Western humanity and the development of modern culture. Christendom stands for the social, cultural, and political embodiment of the Christian faith.

On the other hand, there is what is authentically proper to Christianity (*Christlichkeit*). This refers to the original Christian experience which occurs in a specific historical period of time: the time of the first Christians, *prior to* the writing down of the Gospels and prior to Paul's missionary activities. It is important to further clarify this distinction since it sheds light on the event of the loss of the gods. What became clear concerning the first aspect—namely, that the most fundamental core of this loss of the gods lies in the essence of metaphysics itself—also appears to be the case here.[18]

The pure and original Christianity is a mode of being that lives entirely on *faith*, which is to be understood as a new mode of existence. God is here not understood as a metaphysical principle that is *elsewhere*, but as the one who has entered history in a concrete manner and announces salvation to humankind. Faith is not *Dasein's* project, but something that comes to humankind out of the kerygma. God is believed to be the one who properly acts, elects the community of faith, and who is thereby actively present among mankind. Faith essentially presupposes a *leap* into a bottomless abyss. This means that the attitude of faith only finds its justification in faith itself. Faith is not created by the human being, but it is received, for nothing, it is *grace*.

Over against this there is *Christendom*. Christendom refers to metaphysics and to adaptation to the world. God is inserted into the project of metaphysics and made into a *value*, the highest value. Faith is reduced to a *Weltanschauung* that offers an explanation of the world. It provides an orientation for maintaining oneself in this world. It can also be used as a means to power in a project of political domination. All this lies far from the original Christianity. Whoever fights against Christianity, and thus against faith as a social-political phenomenon or as ideology, does not thus necessarily fight against the original Christian faith.[19] Likewise, a critique of theology is not necessarily a critique of faith. In modernity Christianity loses its original essence. It degenerates into a *Weltanschauung* and takes on the form of a thinking that is essential for metaphysics. This process goes hand in hand with a dedivinization, which is rooted in the essential structure of the metaphysics at work in history.

The Metaphysics of Subjectivity—How might we formulate this loss of the gods more positively? As was evident it is grounded in a pact between metaphysics and Christianity, but what concretely is the effect of that pact?

To clarify this we must look more closely at one of Heidegger's remarkable thoughts. In the cited passage from *The Age of the World Picture,* he writes that the loss of the gods does not exclude religiosity, but on the contrary, it first makes something like religious experience possible. It is thus related to a certain form of religiosity. Stronger still: it seems to realize itself within this form of religiosity. How is that to be understood?

To that end the passage itself is not sufficient. It does, however, indicate the direction in which we must search. The passage implies that there is a fundamental relationship between the loss of the gods brought about by metaphysics and the essence of the modern religion of feeling. With this we are set on the track of a thought that is at first sight unusual. This thought implies that the classic opposition between the God of the Bible and the God of the philosophers is not decisive for the problematic of the loss of the gods. In both of the opposed positions the *same* event takes place. Formulated in yet another way: in Hegel and Kierkegaard one and the same fate is realized.

H. Birault elucidates this thesis as follows.[20] Heidegger describes the religion that goes with the loss of the gods in terms of "religious experience." Here religion undergoes an alteration. The relation to the divine now takes on the shape of an affective formation of human subjectivity. Religion thus loses its objective reference. The relation to God is reduced to a purely subjective matter. God is no longer experienced as present in actuality as such. Actuality loses its sacral dimension. The only remaining place for the divine is in the believing subjectivity. God is now present in feeling, in personal experience, in private religious conviction, in existential pathos.

So one can understand why Heidegger in *The Age of the World Picture* writes that "when this has occurred [namely that religion is changed into religious experience, L.H.] then the gods have fled." The pathos of the pure and authentic religious existence cannot disguise what is taking place. The will to return to a kind of pure and original Christianity, Heidegger holds, cannot withdraw itself from the fate that the history of Being brings. The opposition to metaphysics, to the God of the philosophers, to the Christendom that has become "culture" is not essential. Within the history of Being there is a fundamental relationship between theological metaphysical thought and the antimetaphysical (antispeculative) religiosity of feeling. There is a solidarity in the depths between the point of view of reason and the heart, between the God of the philosophers and the God of Pascal, between Hegel and Kierkegaard. Although the religion of subjectivity protests against the philosophical form of the loss of the gods—namely, against rational metaphysics—it cannot prevent actuality from losing its sacral meaning. The reason is that both the religion of feeling and modern metaphysics are determined by the same logic—namely, the logic of subjectivity. In *Holzwege* Heidegger calls Kierkegaard a religious writer, not just one among others, but the only one in accord with the fate of his time.[21] The time in which Kierkegaard (the preeminent example of religious experience) writes, is the time in which Hegel's metaphysics reigns. Actually, this is still our time: the time in which the domination of metaphysics comes to completion. That is why Kierkegaard and Hegel, the one a religious writer, the other a thinker, have a special actuality for us. Though fundamentally different they belong to one and the same regime, they are touched by the same fate. In different modes—the subjectivity of feeling and pathos in the one, the rational subjectivity in the other—the same event takes place: the dedivinization of the world.

At first glance this is strange. It seems that the religion of subjective experience must be understood as a heroic counterweight to the dedivinization that proceeds apace. In reality it is also the medium in which the loss of the gods occurs.

According to Birault, Heidegger's point of view provides an insight into a remarkable aspect of the relationship between faith and knowing in modernity. There appears to be an essential *solidarity* between the perspective of the *heart* and that of *reason*: *in both the subject becomes the unique locus of the absolute*. Descartes's *idea of the infinite* is the first and decisive stimulus to this solidarity. When we explore the depth of our spiritual interiority we arrives at the idea of God put there by God. Then a process of further interiorization and spiritualization of God takes place, a further intertwining of God and the human spirit (this culminates in different ways, theistic or atheistic, in Hegel and the left-Hegelians). But, and this is now of essential importance for us, this process occurs in two modes: the mode of rational subjectivity in Descartes, Kant, and Hegel; the mode of passionate subjectivity in Pascal, Jacobi, and Kierkegaard. Just as Hegel and Kierkegaard express the same metaphysical principle in different ways, so also do Kant and Jacobi, Descartes and Pascal. This reveals the essential relationship between the essence of metaphysics and the essence of modern religion. In both spheres something more fundamental happens, something more decisive:

the loss of the divine connected to the *onto-theological structure* of metaphysics, and the development of the *principle of subjectivity* which is the principle of the completed form of this metaphysics.

Heidegger writes that this dedivinization results in a void. This void is then filled by a historiographical and psychological investigation of myth. Even this thesis is contrary to the prevailing conception of the loss. The investigation of which Heidegger speaks is the modern scientific analysis and explanation of individual and collective religious representations. As is well known, this investigation is often of a reductive nature. It reduces the specifically religious to a function of other, nonreligious processes. Most often it has a demythologizing tendency. Myth is then unmasked as an archaic remnant.

What is remarkable about Heidegger's thesis is that the dedivinization is not presented as the result of this scientific approach and its reductive mentality. Rather the void resulting from the dedivinization, as it were, creates the space for this reductive scientific activity. The relation to God is now replaced by a scientific explanation of the forms in which this relationship is historically expressed—namely, myths. The scientific explanation is only possible within the void created by the disappearance of the gods, a disappearance grounded in the *essence of metaphysics* itself.

Perhaps these considerations help to some extent to clarify the one sentence in which Heidegger, in the passage cited from *The Age of the World Picture*, positively indicates the fifth distinguishing characteristic of modernity. He writes, "The loss of the gods is the situation of indecision regarding God and the gods." In the German text the word for indecision is *Entscheidungslosigkeit*. In light of the foregoing, the term suggests a possible interpretation of this remarkable description.

The time of the loss of the gods is a time in which thought cannot come to a decision, cannot take up a position with respect to the nature of the divine and its relation to mortals. It is not the right time, knowing that the moment has arrived, to resolutely (*Entschlossen*) dedicate oneself to the affair of the divine. The time of the loss of the gods is a time poor in *kairos*. The opportune moment to become engaged in this matter has not (yet?) arrived. Indeed, this is the age that is dominated by metaphysics, it is the age of nihilism. That is why it is better to keep silent about God and the gods, and to wait. Now is not the opportune time, the kairos.

What is essential here is not that humankind falls short. Its *Entscheidungslosigkeit* is something that happens to it as a fate. It results from the domination of metaphysics. This domination is not caused by *our* thinking, but is rooted *in* the mystery of the history of Being (*Seinsgeschick*) itself. Elsewhere Heidegger writes: "Whether God lives or remains dead is not decided (pay close attention to the term *entscheidet*, L.H.) by human religiosity and even less by the theological aspirations of philosophy and the natural sciences. Whether or not God is God comes disclosingly to pass from out of and within the constellation of Being. So long as we do not, through thinking, experience what is, we can never belong to what will be."[22]

Here the profound meaning of the citation from the *Letter on Humanism*, with which we began this section, shows itself. It is too early to speak about God. However, we can prepare ourselves for a speaking which is more genuine, a nonmetaphysical speaking about God. To this end we must learn to listen and open ourselves up to the word of the poets—and the poet *par excellence*: Hölderlin. They can provide a *hint* as to the direction of the holy, a necessary condition for being able to think God. They can prepare us for a new openness to the holy and so clear the way for access to a nonmetaphysical God.[23]

Thinking Does not Merely "Happen" to Us—This is not the place for an elaborate discussion of Heidegger. It has been repeatedly and abundantly pointed out that his interpretation of the essence and history of metaphysics needs correction.[24]

The experiences that thought can undergo (when it tries to understand the enigma of contingency, the connection between thinking and being, and the ethical ought) do not "automatically" lose their worth with reference to a contestable elucidation of metaphysics. More precise analyses are needed to appreciate these experiences. Great schemes obscure the matter. So we have frequently shown that the experiences of thought that can lead to God and which we have repeatedly reconstructed and construed do not conceive of God as a highest being nor as a scientific principle of explanation.

The challenge to a thinking about God which can emanate from Heidegger's thought lies on another level. It concerns less the specific reconstruction of the history of Western thought as the *systematic position* that is expressed in it, Heidegger's own *ontology* which decisively determines his reading of history.

Heidegger continuously emphasizes the *fateful* character of thought. It is to be understood from the perspective of the diverse *dispensations* that form the history of being (*Seinsgeschichte, Seinsgeschick*).[25] That the gods have fled, that the one-dimensionality of technology dominates, that we can no longer truly think and so on, that, in other words, "we think as we think" is understood by Heidegger as something that *happens to us*. Thought, including thought about God, is at the mercy of an inscrutable play of history. One is sometimes reminded of Hegel, at least of his teleological conception of history. However, in Heidegger we seem to deal with a kind of *reversed* Hegelian conception of history. History is not a "progression in the consciousness of freedom," a process of Spirit's increasing insight into what it is. Rather, it is a history of unhallowing, a process of increasing lack of freedom and darkening until the lowest point of nihilism, in which we "now" live.

Even more important than this conception of history is its relation to thought. Here a comparison with Hegel can also be illuminating. For Hegel history can be dialectically reconstructed. What at first strikes us as a kind of fate can be recuperated by thought. History then ceases to be a blind power. This no longer seems feasible in Heidegger.[26] History becomes an alien agency which withdraws itself from thought. As Heidegger himself formulates it, not *logos*, but *chronos* is the perspective into which history and thought fall. *Chronos* determines and delimits thought in a way that cannot be neutralized. Hence, nothing decisive can be said about the possibility of an *essential* thought of God. It appears to be too early *now* . . . or *always, who knows?* Even this last possibility cannot be excluded, as Heidegger writes (in *Die onto-Theologische Verfassung der Meta-physik*) after a concise characterization of the "other thinking" that is no longer metaphysical or ontological: "Thus the step back would itself remain unaccomplished, and the path which it opens and points out would remain untrod."[27]

Here philosophical thought encounters inexorable limits. It is completely permeated by *time*. *It* thus shares in the *externality* that characterizes time and is completely at the mercy of finitude. Whereas for Hegel the *concept* breaks *the power of time* and neutralizes its characteristic dissemination, time no longer "grants" thinking that form of presence.[28] What remains is *waiting*, a heroic practise of passivity. Waiting until "something" comes, from elsewhere, from outside.

Here Heidegger's thought slides into a sort of *revelational-theological* speech. It is as if Western culture and the science and philosophy essential to that culture have exhausted their strength.

What seems to remain is a waiting—obviously active, attentive, alert for every sign, but nevertheless a waiting—until a *new revelation* takes place. Could this be the meaning of the statement from the controversial *Spiegel* interview: "Only a God can save us"?[29] That must also hold for thinking about God. Will we only be able to essentially think God (anew?) when God (again) is revealed to us?

It is as if the circle of Heidegger's development comes to a close here. Earlier on, religion in the form of Christianity was presented as a unique mode of existence, opposed not only to Christendom, but also to philosophy. Now in the later texts, something is also radically opposed to philosophical (metaphysical) thought. Except now the direction and one side of the opposition are different. The main issues now are the "other thinking" and something that must still realize itself. But what was proper to religion, also holds for this "other," essential, yet to be: it must reveal itself, come to us, as a grace happens us.[30]

Philosophizing is impossible without a radical openness. Without being addressed by something other, by *actuality*, it remains a purely formal movement. Nevertheless, it remains a *thinking for oneself*. That is more than waiting, however actively this may be understood.

Among other things this means that thinking exists by the grace of a *faith* that what happens to us is not in principle inaccessible to understanding. Hence thinking does not come to a standstill at the radical contingency that it has from Heidegger's perspective, and which unmasks every possible ground as an abyss. Contingency is not the only horizon. Indeed in the question of the ground, this is *actually* shown. The finite is finite—that is to say, not absolute.

The question is: Which takes finitude *more* seriously, a thinking which, due to specific experiences, thinks it must move to the absolute, or a thinking which, fascinated by finitude, is unable to realize this movement? Indeed, on this point the proximity to some of Heidegger's thoughts is greater than it might appear from the perspective of our critical evaluation. Undoubtedly a certain experience of *Unheimlichkeit* speaks through Heidegger's texts, an experience of dissatisfaction with the *immediate*. This concerns something that prevents us from establishing ourselves definitively in the *here* and *now*. Is this not a form of resistance against an unqualified acceptance of contingency? That is why Heidegger's thought is continually looking forward to something other. It is a thinking in which the *ontological difference* is the hinge.[31] However, it seems that this other cannot be affirmed by philosophical thought: it withdraws itself from the *concept*. Hence the experience of finitude takes on a *tragic* character in Heidegger. It is reminiscent of an "unhappy consciousness" that knows itself condemned to an orientation toward something which fundamentally withdraws. This is qualitatively different from a "positive atheism."[32] In such an atheism finitude is so absolute that consciousness can no longer feel unhappy, because it is no longer oriented to something other.

In the following, final section of this book the problematic of finitude is further developed. We are guided by the paradoxical thought *"that we are too finite to bear our finitude."*[33] I will give to this thought a somewhat different twist. For us it does not necessarily mean that we need the illusion of God to sustain ourselves in our existence. This formula can also express something else, something which is a decisive experience in philosophical ways toward God.

This consists in the *refusal to absolutize the finite*: our finitude is not a self-sufficient reality. That is why it cannot sustain itself—that is to say, be its own ground *for* itself. This is not because of a kind of speculative illusion or some psychological mechanism or other. It is so on the basis of what *finitude as such is*.

Thinking finitude means understanding that it is grounded in something else. *As finite*, we are thus *always already* beyond the *limit of finitude*.[34] What in the past in a deficient terminology was called *proof* for the existence of God, is the expression of the inescapable *dialectic of finite and infinite* which manifests itself in the thought of finitude. "Proving" God entails making explicit what we are: *finite spirit*.

5.2 THE MYSTERY OF GOD'S PRESENCE

The Death of God—"Is not the greatness of this deed too great for us? Must we ourselves not become gods simply to appear worthy of it?" Thus asks the madman (*der tolle Mensch*) when he proclaims God's "death" to the onlookers who can barely comprehend.[35]

This expression is exemplary of the many passages in Nietzsche's work which articulates the specially problematic character of an important ideal dominating his work—namely, the *absolute acceptance of finitude*. On the one hand, Nietzsche's work is a *diagnosis* of culture. An important facet of this diagnosis is the announcement of nihilism, which is summarized in the death of God. That God is dead means that the highest values that give meaning and orientation to life have lost their value. Western culture has been bled dry. The traditional values, expressed from time immemorial in religion, morality, and metaphysics, no longer inspire life. There is no longer an *aim* to provide life with meaning and direction. There is no longer a great *coherent whole* in which things are embedded and from which individual existence would derive its meaning. There is no longer a *truth* that gives warrant for the essence of beings. There is no longer a *ground* that is the origin and sustainer of all. In this diagnosis Nietzsche seeks to unmask morality, religion, and metaphysics as *symptoms of decadence*: the result of a perverted will to power and of resentment. Religion, morality, and metaphysics are in turn deemed nihilistic, because they have "seduced" humankind to give itself over to a fantastical afterworld (*Hinterwelt*). As a result humankind turns away from the earth, from the "genuine" life. They are "negators of life."

Nietzsche calls Brahmanism, Buddhism, and Christendom nihilistic "because they have all glorified the antithesis of life, nothingness, as goal, as highest good, as God."[36] This nihilism is the ground for ordinary nihilism, in which life becomes meaningless, in which a "great sadness come[s] over humankind" that coincides with the belief that "everything is empty, everything is one, everything is past!"[37]

On the other hand, Nietzsche's work is in a certain way a *therapy*. It tries to overcome nihilism, not by turning away from it or fighting it on the basis of a certain morality, a new type of religion or metaphysics. Nietzsche attempts to overcome nihilism by accepting it absolutely. This leads to a new morality, the tragic-dionysian attitude to life in which existence is affirmed without reservation in its groundlessness, lack of orientation, and valuelessness.[38] The world is eternally chaos and strife. Nietzsche's therapy does not deliver us from this. It urges only that we wholly identify ourselves with it without any reservation.

From this point of view God is merely an interpretation. It is not a false interpretation, because that would still presuppose the metaphysical concept of truth. It is however an interpretation that is too weak to accept and affirm the incompatibility of the conflicting perspectives that characterize existence. This heroic therapy is expressed in the great themes of Nietzsche's work such as the *Übermensch*, the will to power, *amor fati* and the eternal recurrence of the same.

It is almost impossible rationally and thoughtfully to carry through Nietzsche's critique of metaphysics. This is apparent from the fact that, among other things, it is almost impossible to formulate this critique outside of the poetic or aphoristic style.[39] But there is not just a theoretical problem. Perhaps there is a practical and existential question more fundamental to, and more problematic for, the possibility of Nietzsche's entire project.

What the madman proclaims—namely, that the death of God is something that is perhaps too great for the human being—can the human being deny the absolute? This doubt accompanies Nietzsche's ideal as a shadow. Nietzsche's *positive nihilism* is the nihilism of the strong one, of the one who without reserve affirms existence and *all* that it contains, and who is able to endure all the conflicts that existence inevitably brings with it. This nihilism is perhaps the most radical conception of finitude in the history of Western thought. At the same time it seems to be corroded from within by a fundamental doubt about its ultimate possibility.

The human being seems too finite to fully bear its own finitude. To be able to realize the ideal of being its own ground—that is to exist *without ground*—to wholly sustain itself, the human being would have to be a kind of god. But it is not a god. There is no God. Hence, Nietzsche's ideal becomes something impossible, it cannot be achieved by the finite human being. His project fails because of this *contradiction*. It falls victim to what it attempts to ward off. It is nevertheless a *"brilliant failure."*[40]

This failure is grounded in something that dominates Nietzsche's thought like a decision not open to discussion—namely, an *absolutization of finitude*. The cultural diagnosis, in which this absolutization comes to expression, weighs heavily on the therapy and precludes its becoming practical: a way of life that can be lived by the human being.[41] In this diagnosis Nietzsche is not just someone who characterizes his time. In this evaluation of finitude he is likewise the expression of his time.

Nietzsche as Child of his Time—That his thinking is so popular today is no accident. Our time is not only dominated by the logic of the absence of the essential. It is also predominately determined by what paradoxically results from this logic, like a new kind of absolute—namely, the coming to the fore of *finitude* as the *only perspective*.[43] Is not this a *wrongly understood fidelity to finitude*?

There is a form of living and thinking which is indeed *nihilistic*, in that the here and now, the visible and what can be experienced, present actuality itself as having lost weight. This negation can take on diverse forms. It can be a clinging to forms of the past, usually retrospectively modified. It can be an orientation toward the future, toward the other, such that every presence evaporates and existence is reduced to living in the deferral. It can be lived in secular or religious terms. This contingent actuality and its accompanying contingent freedom can be negated both in a flight *up* or a flight *forward*, a flight into a *supernature* or into a *future nature*. The denial can appear as a dualistic spiritualism, or as a moralistic asceticism, in which one only *is* something through a negation of what is. It can also take the form of political terrorism, in which every positivity is destroyed in function of a future absolute end. It can result in forms of pseudo-mystical escapism.

However, genuine fidelity to finitude does not lie in a reversal of this nihilistic position. "Be true to the earth" can never mean making that which is finite into an absolute, *into something which it is not*. Fidelity implies a moment of truth. It is distinguished from a clinging to something illusory or a fixation on something phantastic. Remaining true to the earth cannot mean making it into something that it is not. Fidelity is not only a subjective disposition. It also has an objective referent: it is binding oneself to a person or an issue *as it is*.

Not only is there a world of difference between the full and lucid acceptance of finitude and its absolutization. The latter concerns an unjustifiable leap, because it is essential for the finite that *it is not absolute*. The finite is but finite: this seemingly trivial insight is of critical importance for the question of God.

Here Heidegger's question "How does God enter philosophy?" finds an answer.[44] Thinking God means executing the movement which takes place *in* thinking about this finite actuality. In this book I have tried to reconstruct as well as construct a few of the forms that such a movement can take. Whether these ways are practicable and whether they are appealing (a matter which is *more* than being able to explicate their logic) depends upon the *appreciation of finitude*.

Hegel: The Absolute is Present—God's presence can only be conjectured, when thought frees itself from every *misplaced* tenderness for finitude.[45] This liberation does not necessarily come down to a nihilistic denial of the finite or a flight to a *Hinterwelt* (afterworld). This has been illustrated in a unique way in Hegel's philosophy. His thought moves *on the boundary between the finite and infinite.* Boundary here refers more to what unites rather than divides. For Hegel, the idea that the finite is but finite means that it is also always beyond the boundary. It is not a self-sufficient actuality resting in itself.

In one of his *Lectures on the Proofs for the Existence of God* Hegel calls "this . . . way of dealing with the nature of the finite . . . the pivot round which the whole question, namely, as to the knowledge of God . . . turns."[46] The finite can only play its mediating role if one gives full weight to what it is and in no way veils its finitude.

According to Hegel this particular evaluation of finitude constitutes the fundamental principle of idealism. In *The Science of Logic* he writes "the proposition that the finite is ideal [*Ideell*] constitutes idealism."[47] That the finite is ideal, means that it is defined as the "temporal, the contingent, the changeable and transitory."[48] Although it *is*, it is not in *the* fully affirmative sense of the word. Its being is not self-sufficient. It must be determined as that which sublates and negates itself. It is affected from within by a negativity whereby it is subject to contradictions and hence dissolves and passes away. It does not succeed in maintaining itself definitively in its existence.[49]

Elsewhere Hegel calls this typical mode of being of the finite the *dialectical character* of the finite.[50] This indicates that the finite is the process of *transition* to the infinite. This transition reveals that the finite must be understood as a *moment* of the absolute. It is likewise clear that this conception of finitude does not lead to a dualism in which the finite world would stand over on one side confronting an infinite, true world.

Indeed, what is essential for the finite is that it cannot maintain itself over and against the absolute. It does not stand over against the infinite as though independent, "it is not its own Being, but is, on the contrary, the Being of its other, namely, the Infinite."[51] It is only a *moment.* That is why Hegel calls it ideal.

According to him, that idealistic principle is not only proper to idealistic philosophy *stricto sensu*, distinguished from other types of philosophy, such as realism for example. Every philosophy is in some way idealistic. Indeed, in a philosophy one does not stop at beings as they are immediately presented to consciousness, such as stones, plants, people, planets, cultural objects, states, languages, values, and so on. On the contrary, one poses questions about each of these things. One wants to understand and discover connections. Philosophy does not consider the immediately apparent reality to be something ultimate. It is conceived as something which lends itself to being understood, and not as senseless and simple facticity. By way of this understanding one breaks through the immediacy of being. One goes further toward something more fundamental, something that reigns and determines the multitude of beings. That which is fundamental is not an immediate being that can be apprehended by the senses.

In so called idealistic philosophy, this principle, which characterizes all forms of philosophy (and really also science), is thought through to the utmost.[52] All that is, is understood as a moment of the idea, as a moment of an encompassing intelligible essence which rests in itself.[53] This is not an anonymous rational structure but a living actuality. Due to its free and self-conscious character this rational essence must be called *Spirit*.

That the finite is, in fact ideal, does not mean that it is not real or only a sort of representation. Ideal has an objective connotation. Indeed, idea stands for Being in its most perfect mode of being, for actuality in its highest actualization. The idea is not merely a subjective conception. It is the rational totality which supports and encompasses all subjectivity and objectivity.

In relation to this actuality the finite is not something independent. It is dialectical, which means that it is a moment of the Absolute, it is a transition to the infinite. To think the finite adequately means to execute this process of transition in a conceptual mode.

Hegel's entire philosophy consists in this conceptual movement. One could call it the process wherein spirit elevates itself to the Absolute. Or formulated from another point of view: the process in which what spirit *is* is conceptually realized—namely, elevation (*Erhebung*) to the absolute as to its deepest essence.

Hegel says that what were traditionally called proofs for the existence of God, must be understood as illustrations of *such a conceptual elevation* that spirit *is*. What happens in *religion* in the medium of feeling and representation occurs in these proofs by way of thought. Proofs for the existence of God "succeed" if and only if the dialectic of finitude is adequately developed in it, if the finitude of the finite is in no way obscured. The finite must be understood as what it is: a movement to the Absolute of which it is a moment.

The classic metaphysical proofs for God are, according to Hegel, inadequate explanations of this elevation.[54] Their shortcoming consists primarily in the fact that they do not express the moment of *negation* which is, as we have seen, essential to this elevation. Their logical form—namely the syllogism—conceals the negation that is inherent in this elevation. This form expresses a discursive process, which starts from some finite content which is then *affirmatively* maintained throughout the argument. One moves from one positivity to the other: from the world (the human being) to God. Here thinking remains bound to the form of the understanding, to empirical data, to finitude.

In this context Hegel calls Kant's critique of the traditional proofs for the existence of God justified: "It is accordingly of the greatest importance that Kant should have deprived the so-called proofs of the existence of God of the regard they enjoyed."[55] But Kant did not discern the more fundamental foundation of these proofs. He did not valorize the dynamic of reason which expresses itself in this inadequate form. This only happens when full weight is given to the negativity that is essential to the finite.

In a real elevation to God one does not stop at the empirical. Indeed, what is *present-to-hand* is *thought* in such an elevation. It becomes something universal: "By the removal and negation of the shell, the kernel within the sense-percept is brought to the light."[56] This implies a moment of negativity, in which finitude, nullity, the "happen-stance" of the contingent world is brought to the light. The *elevation* (*Erhebung*) is a going beyond (*hinausgehen*). The proof contains a break with the finite world. It brings to expression "that the being of the world only has a semblance, no real being" and that "unless the being of the world is nullified, the *point d'appui* for the exaltation is lost" ("*nur die Nichtigkeit des Seins der Welt ist das Band der Erhebung*").[57]

Of course, this negativity as such is not sufficient. *Without a presence of God in the finite the elevation would be even less of a possibility*. The elevation can only occur because the finite is a moment of the infinite. The elevation implies the fundamental *unity of thought and being* which is expressed in the *ontological* proof. The finite is a moment of the infinite. As a moment it is simultaneously denied *and* affirmed, limited and driven beyond its limits. If there were only negativity, if the negativity were not dialectical but rather absolute, then only the absolute vanity and groundlessness of all that is would remain. Then every elevation should just fall away.

Whoever fully valorizes finitude—something different to absolutizing it—is thereby always *beyond its limits*. One might retort that the transcending movement beyond the limits, although unavoidable, terminates neither in something absolute nor in God.

Must finitude not be taken seriously to such an extent *that the transcendence proper to it*, that its transcendental openness, *is itself finite*? Must what is thought in Hegel's metaphysics be now interpreted anthropologically as *finite transcendence*?

Finite Transcendence?—Not long after Hegel's death attempts were made to bring to light the truth of Hegel's great metaphysical synthesis by reducing his thought about the absolute to an anthropological thesis. This was the core, for example, of Bruno Bauer's 1841 text *Die Posaune des jüngsten Gerichts über Hegel den Atheisten und Antichristen*.[58] According to Bauer, understanding Hegel's philosophy about the absolute involves carrying out two unmaskings. First and foremost, his *theism*, which gives the impression of understanding God as a person, must be unmasked as a *pantheism*. Then this pantheism must be exposed as an *atheism*. All *theology is anthropology*. All knowledge of God is knowledge in which humankind expresses and understands *itself*.

Bauer's text itself has not had much historical influence. Nevertheless, its fundamental thesis can be considered as paradigmatic for the rest of the nineteenth century and our own time.[59] However, my main concern is not with the history of this *anthropological turn*. I limit myself to the systematic position it expresses.

Human transcendence is finite but simultaneously moves beyond every limit. However, does this openness justify the affirmation of an absolute actuality, thought to be the ground and the end of that movement? Can God, as the one who fulfils this movement, not be unmasked as a phantastic closing off of the openness of *desire*? God as *the* ultimate object, the thing itself, who as the fulfillment would also be the destruction of desire's open dynamic? Against this must we not claim that accepting finitude implies holding the openness of desire open—that is, to be without ground or telos? Then our transcendence does not "prove" our being in God. It only signals the dialectical structure of desire.

That this position is something real is clearly apparent from humankind's current self-understanding. Nevertheless, the following considerations impose themselves on us from the way followed in this book.

From the analysis of the experiences that can lead thought to an affirmation of God, it became clear that God is not understood as a great, phantastic fulfillment of the openness of desire.

On the contrary, the "God of the philosophers" is thought as an actuality that exceeds every finite measure. God's transcendence resists inclusion in the framework of different projections that arise out of desire. *God does not answer to a need.*[60] God must be understood as the ground of desire's dialectical structure instead of its fulfillment. Descartes has emphazised this like no other: in the idea of the infinite the ideatum surpasses the idea of it in us. This thought finds a religious expression in Jewish prophetism. The God of the prophets is not the sacral fulfillment of a need. On the contrary: God breaks through the entrenched structure of need and invites an openness hitherto unsuspected.[61] God does not "solve" the "problem" of finitude. Finite being is a moment of the absolute, not the absolute itself. God neither fulfills finitude nor closes it off.[62] Yet God is revealed as the ground of its possibility. As transcendental ground this ground remains fundamentally *mysterious*. However, and this is the "truth" of Hegel's "experience: *it is mystery "of" this finitude itself.*

Philosophy's Claim to Truth—Is finitude not more respected and recognized in its essence in agnosticism? Is this not more in accordance with our *condition humaine?*

From the foregoing it will have become clear that *my* answer to these questions is negative.

However, this claim to truth goes with the awareness that there are many positions with respect to the problematic of God.

In the foregoing I have continually spoken of *experiences* that thought *can* go through. They do not remain mere possibilities. I have illustrated their reality by way of historical examples. I have further developed them in my own manner. I have ascertained that the insights resulting from these experiences have a *claim* to truth. They were not merely an *opinion* about reality. The aim was to say *what* is.

Here philosophy appears to be something paradoxical: directed toward *universality* it consists of a multiplicity of *particular* positions. Of course, one can be mistaken. A position is not per definition true because it is expressed with full conviction, as something very personal. One can philosophize better or worse, there are stronger and weaker positions, there are great thinkers and there are those who, like us, still try to see something "like dwarfs seated on the shoulders of giants."

Although not every attempt at saying *what is* is at the same time *true*, there nevertheless remains a limit that cannot be surpassed, which is given by the *paradoxical particularity of philosophical universality*.

So one can think, and know oneself forced to accept, that an adequate concept of finitude leads to the affirmation of God. One can also experience not being able to, or allowed to, complete this movement, and therefore not able to consider finitude as contained in the mystery of God's presence. We have followed the first way, guided by a multiplicity of experiences from the philosophical tradition. The commitment to truth nevertheless necessitates continually keeping in mind the other possibilities also expressed in many texts.

Does this not indicate that philosophy in its deepest roots is actually a form of "faith"? Or is thought so interwoven with particular, prephilosophical experiences, that the universality of philosophical truth claims remains an everlasting task? Does this finally mean "to each his truth"?

Philosophy—every philosophy—opposes such a radical pluralism: it wants to say the truth and not just a personal opinion or an interesting point of view. At the same time it knows itself as saturated by an incontrovertible multiplicity. In addition, it knows that this multiplicity is not to be valued negatively. What would be the state of philosophy if truth had to be thought as complete presence, without any reserve, any mystery, any refraction of the absolute, of reality as it *is*? Would this blinding light not make all sight impossible? *Who* would then still think?

Philosophy exists by the grace of an enigmatic interlacing of unity and multiplicity in the truth. This interwovenness is not a problem that can be solved. It points to the mystery of reality itself whose inexhaustible depths motivate thought to endless activity.

Indeed, the multiplicity of truth does not just signify a plurality of individual standpoints. It is not only something external. It does not just fall apart into a plurality of clearly traceable standpoints or theories. Indeed, positions can sometimes compete with each other and pass over into each other from the opposing point of view. But above all: *the plurality is something that resides in one's ownmost individuality. It characterizes one's ownmost thought in many ways. The one who thinks differently is not merely someone thinking differently. He is also in myself.*

That is why the philosophical position developed in the foregoing is more a task than a solution. It is a task for thinking, for the exchange of ideas with others and for a never-ending conversation of the soul with itself.

Notes

INTRODUCTION

1. This expression is taken from Theo De Boer's *De God van de filosofen en de God van Pascal* [The God of the Philosophers and the God of Pascal], The Hague 1989, pp. 59–60.

2. This problematic is further developed in Chapter 5.

3. Aristotle, *Metaphysics* A.

4. The term *experiences of thought* plays an important role in what follows. It refers to what Hegel calls the experience of *consciousness* in the introduction to *The Phenomenology of Spirit*. This is further developed in the first section of the second chapter under the title "The experience of thought."

5. Following Hegel's critique of a too onesided emphasis on the critique of knowledge (in the introduction to *The Phenomenology of Spirit*).

6. Kant, *Critique of Pure Reason*, B 294. Translated by Norman Kemp Smith, Macmillan, London, 1992, p. 257.

7. The term theology here means nothing more than "a conception of God." It does not refer to a particular scholarly discipline.

8. This expression is a variation on Hegel's famous saying in the preface to the *Philosophy of Right*; what is rational is actual, and what is actual is rational.

CHAPTER ONE

1. Descartes, *Méditations*, ed. Pléiade, p. 267. English translation by John Cottingham, *Descartes' Meditations*, Cambridge University Press, 1996, p. 12.

2. What follows is not an exegesis of the pertinent sections of the *Phenomenology*. As I said, the text is "used" with a view to the clarification of a systematic problematic. This means that my concern is not with the role this text plays in the whole of Hegel's work.

3. The function of the *Phenomenology* in the development of Hegel's system is outside my current concerns.

4. In interpreting Hegel's text I make frequent use of: P.J. Labarrière, *Introduction à une lecture de le Phénoménologie de l'esprit de Hegel*, Paris, 1979; J. Hyppolite, *Genèse et structure de la Phénoménologie de l'esprit de Hegel*, Paris, 1978: A. Léonard, *La foi chez Hegel*, Paris, 1970.

5. *Phänomenologie des Geistes* (ed. Philos. Bibl. 1952[6]), pp. 358 ff. Translated into English by A.V. Miller *Hegel's Phenomenology of Spirit*, 1977, Clarendon Press, Oxford, pp. 305ff. For an interpretation of the problematic of alienation, see also C.Boey, *L'aliénation dans la phénoménologie de l'esprit*,Paris-Bruges,1970.

6. Ibid., pp. 372–73 (English translation, pp. 317–18).

7. In Hegel's text faith concerns Christian faith. Other forms of religious faith lie outside consideration.

8. Here I loosely follow the systematic characterization of faith provided by A. Léonard in *La foi chez Hegel*, Paris, 1970, pp. 87–171.

9. *Phänomenologie des Geistes*, p. 379 (English translation, p. 324).

10. Ibid., p. 383 (English translation, p. 328).

11. Ibid., p. 385 (English translation, p. 330).

12. Ibid., p. 387 (English translation, p. 331). Last italics mine.

13. Ibid., p. 388 (English translation, p. 332). In Diderot, *Le Neveu de Rameau*, ed. Gallimard (collection Folio), 1972, p. 105. Translated into English and edited by Jacques Barzun and Donald O'Gorman, *Rameau's Nephew*, Geneva, 1973.

14. *Phänomenologie des Geistes*, p. 388 (English translation, p. 332).

15. Ibid., pp. 391–92 (English translation, p. 335).

16. Ibid., 390 (English translation, p. 334).

17. A. Léonard, *L. foi*, 105.

18. Recall the *logic of understanding* in which the enlightenment is imprisoned, and by means of which it is not in a position to understand religion in its distinctiveness: sheer creation *or* pure givenness, merely from without or exclusively from within.

19. *Phänomenologie des Geistes*, p. 407 (English translation, p. 349).

20. Reason (*Vernunft*) on the other hand is the principle of unity and unification. For an overall characterization of the relation between understanding (*Verstand*) and reason (*Vernunft*), see L. Heyde, *De verwerkelijking van de vrijheid. Een inleiding in Hegel's rechtsfilosofie*, Maastricht/Leuven, 1987, pp. 15–46.

21. Contract-theory has remained the dominant political theory up to

this day. It is in part continued in forms of consensual-thought; in this connection see O. Höffe, *Strategien der Humanität*, Freiburg/Munich, 1975, and L. Heyde, *Staat en Maatschappelijk Contract*, in G. Van Velthoven, *Overheidsbemoeienis*, Deventer, 1982, pp. 3–20.

22. Diderot, *Le Neveu*, p. 126. On the loss of substantiality of the ironic subjectivity, see L. Heyde, "Gebroken Zedelijkheid" (broken ethical life), *Tijdschrift voor filosofie*, 57 (1996).

23. This logic of absence is a major point of reference in the leading philosophies of today. One thinks, for example, of the works of Nietzsche, Derrida, Rorty, Heidegger, and even Levinas. It is clear that the motif of absence plays a role here in various ways. In his valedictory address in Nijmegen on February 21, 1986, Jan Hollak gives an analogous diagnosis of modern culture as standing under the hegemony of the hypothetical.

24 The term "phenomenology" refers here to Hegel, not to the *Phenomenology* as it is initiated by Husserl.

CHAPTER 2

1. As the reader can determine from what follows, we have a different conception of the relation between the "God of philosophy" and the "God of the Bible" than the one worked out by Theo de Boer in his *The God of the Philosophers and the God of Pascal*. De Boer's theory is not only the expression of a conception of faith with a Barthian signature. It is also the result of a philosophical interpretation of the relation between thought and faith, which continues the classical Enlightenment opposition between them. I attempt to overcome this opposition in the sense that what is thought in the "God of the philosophers" is the minimal condition which the "God of faith" must meet in order to have actuality. A more detailed consideration of the relation between them demands a separate study.

2. As will become evident, I limit myself to the Judaeo-Christian form of religiosity. The reason is not one of a principle but is of a *factual* nature: this is the only form of religion of which I have a real historical experience and concerning which I have sufficient knowledge to be able speak of it.

3. Although life and worldviews contain a core which can be expressed philosophically, they are clearly of another nature and fulfill a different function than philosophical theories. In relation to this, see for instance Heidegger's analysis in *Die Grundprobleme der Phänomenologie*, Gesamtausgabe, Band 24, pp. 15–19 (English translation by Albert Hofstadter, *Basic Problems of Phenomenology*, Bloomington, Indiana University

Press, 1982, pp. 11–14); also Husserl's *Philosofie als strenge Wissenschaft* (translated into English as "Philosophy as Rigorous Science" in Q. Lauer, ed. *Phenomenology and the Crisis of Philosophy*, New York, 1965, pp. 71–147). For a contemporary example of a hermeneutic that attempts to clarify the nature of religion and religious language, see C.A. van Peursen, *De Naam die geschiedenis maakt: het geheim van de bijbelse godsnamen*, Kampen, 1991. In addition it is, of course, necessary to refer to the work of A. Vergote, for example, his *Interprétation du language religieux*, Paris, 1974.

4. According to Anselm of Canterbury's famous formulation, in the *Proslogion* (Dutch translation, C. Steel, reeks Dixit, Bussum/Antwerp, 1981, p. 35). English translation, J. Hopkins and H. Richardson, volume one in the series *Anselm of Canterbury*, Edwin Mellen Press, 1974, p. 90.

5. According to N. Hinske in H. Lübbe (Hrsg.), *Wozu Philosophie?* Berlin-New York, 1978, p. 313.

6. Descartes, *Méditations* (ed. Pléiade), p. 267; English translation, p. 12.

7. See Hegel, *The Phenomenology of Spirit, Introduction*; compare also L. Van der Kerken, *Inleiding tot de fundamentele filosofie*, Kapellen, 1969, pp. 13–18.

8. See chapter 5, first section.

9. On this, see H. Cramer, *Gottesbeweise und ihre Kritik*, Frankfurt am Main, 1967, p. 7.

10. I will often come back to the meaning of this frequently misinterpreted term, particularly in section 2 of chapter 5.

11. Philosophy is always, in one way or another, a break with what is common and self-evident, here referred to by the term "natural attitude," a term borrowed from Husserl; see E. Husserl, *Ideen I*, Den Haag, 1976, pp. 56–66; translated into English by F. Kersten, *Ideas pertaining to a Pure Phenomenology and to a Phenomenological Philosophy. First Book: General Introduction to a Pure Phenomenology*, The Hague, 1982, pp. 51–62.

12. See Leibniz, *Principes de la nature et de la grâce*, Opera, ed. Gerhardt, t. VI, 602, nr. 7–8 (translated into English by Roger Ariew and Daniel Garber, *Principles of Nature and Grace, Based on Reason*, in: *G.W. Leibniz: Philosophical Essays*, Hackett, 1989, pp. 206–13); M. Heidegger, *Einführung in die Metaphysik*, Tübingen, 1987⁵, p. 1 (translated into English by Ralph Manheim, *An Introduction to Metaphysics*, London, 1959, p. 1).

13. Among others, see J. Ritter's article "Gottesbeweis" in *Historisches Wörterbuch der Philosophie*.

14. I will return to the problematic suggested by the word *can* in section 2 of chapter 5.

15. Thomas Aquinas, *Summa Theologiae*, I, II, Art. 3. For an analysis and commentary of Thomas's text, see F. van Steenbergen, *Le problème de l'existence de Dieu dans les écrits de St. Thomas d'Aquin*, Louvain-la-Neuve, 1980, pp. 187–205.

16. "Possibile" should here be understood as the contingent—namely, what is but is not necessarily. It is distinguished from the usual meaning of possible—namely, that which is not contradictory.

17. What it presupposes is, among other things, a certain worldview (teleological instead of mechanical), the invalidity of an infinite regression, and, naturally, the metaphysical conception of a suprasensible world.

18. "Taking into account all differences": Thomas's argument concerns *physical* beings. I relate contingency to all beings.

19. Leibniz, *Principes*, pp. 7–8.

20. Heidegger, *Die Grundprobleme*, p. 1.

21. According to B. Welte, *Religionsphilosophie*, Freiburg-Basel-Vienna, 1978, p. 98.

22. Ibid., p. 102.

23. To saying that God *is* the ground is to make God, as Heidegger would say, into a being (a highest being). This unavoidable logic, however, may not harm the qualitative difference between God's being and that of finite beings. In what follows this difference will be shown in diverse ways. However, it is not to be interpreted to mean that God can no longer be understood as the (mysterious) *ground* of beings. That God is not a being among beings means that God is in an eminent manner: God is to be thought of as *actual* in an absolute sense. This is frequently indicated in my text by the term the *Absolute*.

24. I am here following H. Cramer's line of reasoning, *Gottesbeweise*, p. 43. The condition for the validity of this line of reasoning is that time be understood as more than the subjective form of sensible intuition. As becomes clear from Hegel's interpretation of time, in which he develops this "more," time does not thereby become a "container" (*Behälter*) of all things.

25. Kant clearly saw this! See chapter 3. Indeed, the term "ontological" proof stems from Kant, according to B. Weissmahr, *Philosophische Gotteslehre*, Stuttgart, 1983, p. 94.

26. Anselm, *Proslogion*, translation C. Steel, pp. 48–49 (English translation, p. 93).

27. The significance of something does not coincide with its genealogy.

28. Anselm, *Proslogion*, pp. 49–55 (English translation, pp. 93–94).

29. Emphasis mine.

30. The first sentence of chapter 3, with which the quotation ends, adds something essential to chapter 2. If in chapter 2 the existence of God was affirmed, then in chapter 3 this existence is more fully described as to its mode of existence: God exists necessarily, which is more perfect than mere contingent being (thus C. Steel, in his commentary on the text, p. 54).

31. The "fool" refers to Psalm 13(14), I; see Anselm, *Proslogion*, p. 50 (commentary by C. Steel).

32. Also present in a certain sense in Anselm is what D. Henrich (in *Der ontologische Gottesbeweis*, Tübingen, 1967, pp. 3–4) calls the second type of ontological proof, based on the notion of necessity, besides the first type based on the concept of perfection.

33. Anselm, *Proslogion*, Discussion with Gaunilo, pp. 135–36, 150–51 (English translation, pp. 118–19, 127–127).

34. Anselm, *Proslogion*, p. 91; see C. Steel's commentary on p. 48. (English translation of text only, not commentary, p. 104).

35. Heidegger is very explicit about this in *Nietzsche II*, Pfullingen, 1961, pp. 141–73 (translated into English by Frank A. Capuzzi, San Francisco, 1982, pp. 96–123).

36. Here I am following Stegmaier's overall characterization in his book *Substanz. Grundbegriff der Metaphysik*, Stuttgart-Bad Cannstatt, 1977, particularly pp. 85–92.

37. For a historical analysis, see M. Karskens, "The Development of the Opposition, Subjective versus Objective in the 18th century, in *Archiv für Begriffsgeschichte*, 35 (1992), pp. 214–56.

38. Stegmaier, *Substanz*, pp. 85–86, mentions nominalism and the new mathematical physics as the most important motives.

39. Henrich, *Gottesbeweis*, pp. 131–36.

40. Descartes, *Méditations*, ed. *Pléiade*, p. 285 (English translation, p. 25).

41. According to W. Schulz, *Der Gott der neuzeitlichen Metaphysik*, Pfullingen, 1957, p. 33.

42. The second "account" will be the fifth meditation in which the classic ontological proof is developed.

43. Descartes, *Méditations*, p. 278 (English translation, p. 19).

44. Ibid., pp. 288–89 (English translation, pp. 27–29).

45. Ibid., p. 289 (English translation, p. 28).

46. Ibid., p. 294 (English translation, p. 31).

47. Ibid., pp. 294–95 (English translation, p. 31–32).

48. See the *Objections avec les réponses de l'auteur*, particularly the second and third sections.

49. Descartes, *Méditations*, p. 294 (English translation, p. 31).

50. *Objections*, ed. *Pléiade*, p. 361 (English translation, p. 82).

51. Descartes, *Méditations*, p. 312 (English translation, p. 46).

52. Ibid., pp. 312–13 (English translation, p. 46).

53. For the *status quaestionis*, see D. Henrich, *Gottesbeweis*, pp. 73–131.

54. According to D. Henrich, *Gottesbeweis*, pp. 16–20, it is the transition from the idea of perfection to that of the highest power of being which enables Descartes to parry the objections.

55. W. Schulz, *Metaphysik*, p.9.

56. Ibid., p. 9.

57. Ibid., p. 37.

58. Ibid., p. 39.

59. Ibid.

60. Heraclitus, B45 in Diels, *Fragmenten der Vorsokratiker I*, Berlin, 1956 (English translation, of and commentary on Heraclitus by T.M. Robinson, *Heraclitus: Fragments*, Toronto, 1987, nr. 45, p. 33). Herman Berger brought this saying to my attention in his *Zo wijd als alle werkelijkheid*, Baarn, 1977, p. 9. He has also inspired me on other points. It is not always easy to determine what you have received through many years of contact with someone. This does not diminish the fact that within the same fundamental metaphysical orientation the differences between us are not inconsiderable. While he approaches matters more from an Aristotelian-Thomistic tradition, my line of approach to metaphysics and the problem of God is determined more by Hegel. In addition, there are specific points of difference, which will become clear in what follows, particularly in relation to the conception of God in relation to the problem of evil.

61. Aristotle, *De Anima*, III, 8, 431b, 21; Thomas Aquinas, *In Aristotelis librum De Anima*, Liber III, Lectio XIII.

62. A. Peperzak, *Erotiek*, Nijmegen, 1992. The dynamic which is developed in this text also determines one of Peperzak's first works, *Verlangen. De huidige mens en de vraag naar heil*, Bilthoven, 1971.

63. The following is not a mere repetition of what J.L. Chrétien writes in *L'inoubliable et l'inespéré*, Paris, 1991, pp. 9–55. Rather my aim is to make his interpretation of anamnesis fruitful for the present problematic.

CHAPTER 3

1. Kant, *Critique of Pure Reason* (CPR), B641.
2. CPR, B294–295.
3. CPR, *Preface*, First edition, A VII.
4. This play on words is taken from a play on words by Marx on the name Feuerbach: fiery brook, in *Luther als Schiedsrichter zwischen Strauss und Feuerbach*, in K. Marx and F. Engels, *Werke I*, Dietz Verlag, Berlin, 1974, p. 27 (translated into English by D. McLellan, "Luther as Judge between Strauss and Feuerbach," in *Karl Marx: Early Texts*, Basil Blackwell, Oxford, 1972, p. 25)—"Feuerbach is the purgatory of the present time."
5. CPR, B626.
6. This is clearly an allusion to Descartes.
7. CPR, B621–622.
8. CPR, B622.
9. Starting at, CPR, B623 ff.
10. CPR, B624.
11. CPR, B626.
12. CPR, B106.
13. See section 2 in this chapter.
14. CPR, B626.
15. The term *experience* here has a much more limited meaning than in the expression *experience of thought* which I have used frequently. In Kant it means a sensible knowing determined by the activity of understanding.
16. CPR, B629.
17. Ibidem.
18. CPR, B630.
19. CPR, B637.
20. CPR, B632.
21. Ibidem.
22. CPR, B633–634.
23. CPR, B634.
24. CPR, B636.
25. CPR, B637.
26. CPR, idem.
27. In this connection see Kant's treatment of the fourth cosmological antinomy.
28. CPR, B641.
29. CPR, B648.

30. What follows is a free paraphrase of CPR, B650–651.

31. CPR, B655–656.

32. CPR, B658.

33. I limit myself to the idea of God. Kant's "destruction" of the *I* and the world lie outside my considerations.

34. CPR, B391.

35. CPR, B596.

36. CPR, B601.

37. Ibidem.

38. CPR, B606.

39. CPR, B383.

40. CPR, B380.

41. CPR, B672.

42. CPR, B310, B669.

43. CPR, B669.

44. Ibidem.

45. CPR, B668.

46. H. Heine, *Zur Geschichte der Religion und Philosophie in Deutschland* (1834) (Dutch translation: *Religie en Filosofie in Duitsland*, Amsterdam, 1964, p. 96).

47. That Kant himself, given his limited conception of experience, does not use the term "experience," speaks for itself.

48. In a certain sense, because the utilitarian moment (considered as part of the logic of absence in chapter 1), does not play a role here (unless in a negative sense, as that which is subject to critique by the ethical relation). The "success" of Levinas's thought in part affirms our hypothesis concerning absence. The metaphysics which seems to most appeal today is a metaphysics of alterity and difference, a metaphysics of a one-sided conception (because it lacks an immanent moment) of transcendence. Levinas's hard opposition between ontology and metaphysics is a striking illustration of this.

49. The history of German Idealism (Fichte, Schelling, Hegel) must here remain outside present consideration.

50. My interpretation of Kant is in large measure influenced by the research of M. Moors, particularly his doctoral dissertation, *De Godsidee bij Kant. Haar bepalingsstructuur in de voorkritische en kritische transcendentaalfilosofie*, Leuven 1986.

51. *Kritik der praktischen Vernunft, Vorrede* (editie Vorlander, Philosophische Bibliothek, 1967[9]), p. 8 (cited below as KPV). English translation: *Critique of Practical Reason, Preface*, edited and translated by Lewis White Beck, Macmillan, 1993[3], p. 8.

52. KPV, *Analytik VI, Anmerkung*, p. 35 (English translation, p. 30). The central role of the doctrine about the *Faktum* is clearly explained in W. Perreijn, *Kants ethiek tussen ervaring en apriori*, Tilburg, 1993, pp. 186–286.

53. KPV, p. 35 (English translation, p. 30).

54. J. De Visscher, *De immorele mens*, Bilthoven, 1975, pp. 19–34.

55. I. Kant, "Über den Gemeinspruch: Das mag in der Theorie richtig sein, taugt aber nicht für die Praxis, in: *Kleinere Schriften zu Geschichtsphilosophie, Ethik und Politik* (ed. Philos. Bibliothek, 1973), p. 83. Translated into English by E.B. Ashton, *On the Old Saw: That May be Right in Theory but it Won't Work in Practice*, Philadelphia, 1974, p. 54.

56. For what follows, see KPV, pp. 127ff. (English translation, pp. 116ff.).

57. KPV, p. 143 (English translation, p.131).

58. KPV, pp. 127–28 (English translation, pp. 116–117).

59. KPV, p. 141 (English translation, p. 129).

60. KPV, p. 152 (English translation, p. 139).

61. KPV, p. 145 (English translation, pp. 132–33).

62. KPV, p. 35: see also p. 182 (English translation, p. 30: see also p. 165).

63. This is unacceptable in Kant's "rationalistic" worldview.

64. Hegel, *Phänomenologie des Geistes, Einleitung*, p. 64 (English translation, *Introduction*, p. 47).

65. Ibidem, pp. 64–65.

66. This is an allusion to one of the terms used by W. Weischedel to characterize the only doctrine of God still possible in a nihilistic era. See his *Der Gott der Philosophen*, Darmstad, 1983², volume II, pp. 230ff.

67. Hegel, *Enzyklopadie*, par. 51, *Anmerkung* (Part One of the *Enzyklopadie* translated into English by T. F. Geraets, W. A. Suchting, and H. S. Harris, *The Encyclopaedia Logic*, Hackett Publishing Company, Indianapolis, 1991, §51).

68. See W. Schultz, interpretation in *Metaphysik*, pp. 78–85.

69. CPR, B641.

70. Hegel, *Wie der gemeine Menschenverstand die Philosophie nehme* in *Werke in zwanzig Banden (Theorie Werkausgabe Suhrkamp)*, dl. 2, p. 195. Translated into English by H.S. Harris, *How the Ordinary Human Understanding Takes Philosophy*, in *Between Kant and Hegel: Texts in the Development of Post-Kantian Idealsm*, translated and annotated by George di Giovanni and H.S. Harris, SUNY Press, 1985, 292–310, p. 299.

CHAPTER 4

1. E. Levinas, *Totalité et Infini*, La Haye, 1961, p. 215.

2. *Idem* (For the translation, of both citations I follow Alphonso Lingis in his translation of *Totalité et Infini*, Duquesne University Press, 1969, p. 238).

3. Ibidem, p. 211 (English translation, p. 233).

4. P. Levi, *Is dit een mens?*, Amsterdam, 1988⁵, p. 123.

5. Ibidem., p. 99.

6. Voltaire, *Candide*, Bantam Book, 1984, p. 120.

7. Ibidem.

8. According to R. Spaemann, "Die Frage nach der Bedeutung des Wortes "Gott" [The question of the meaning of the word God], in *Internationale Katholische Zeitschrift*, 1(1972) 62.

9. This classic thesis is worked out by, among others, D. F. Scheltens in *De tijd van God*, Antwerp, 1972, pp. 159–65.

10. See L. De Raeymaeker, *De Metafysiek van het zijn*, Antwerp-Nijmegen, 1947, pp. 245–46.

11. Unless it is the effect of an inconsistent subjectivism, which in the first instance calls all actuality bad, but in a second instance, makes an exception of itself and its own excellence.

12. See the experiment with the "Experience machine," in A. Burms and H. De Dijn, *De Rationaliteit en haar grenzen*, Leuven/Assen/Maastricht, 1986, p. 2.

13. Formulated in Hegel's terminology: the *Aufhebung* is never completely successful.

14. For example, see Plato, *Gorgias*, 492d–501d.

15. The close relationship between "physical" evil (for example, sickness or affliction) and ethics (the unique value of the human person) is revealed, among other things, in the practice of medicine. Only in relation to the human person and its sacrosanct status can physical processes appear as something negative that is to be fought against. Outside of such an association these processes have a "neutral" significance. In any case they do not motivate therapeutic intervention: they are what they are.

16. Thomas Aquinas, *Summa contra Gentiles*, d. 3, c. 71. (English translation, by Vernon J. Bourke, Notre Dame/London, 1975, pp. 240–41). See also D.F. Scheltens, *De tijd van God*, p. 161.

17. In spite of all the opposition between Adorno and Heidegger, there is here a remarkable agreement: history is an "unholy history" and onto-theology has come to an end.

18. Horkheimer and Adorno, *Dialektik der Aufklärung*, Frankfurt am Main, 1984, pp. 59–63. (English translation, by J. Cumming, *Dialectic of Enlightenment*, Herder and Herder, 1972, pp. 43–47). See also W. Van Reijen, *Filosofie als Kritiek*, Alphen a/d Rijn/Brussel, 1981, in particular pp. 122–34, 173–224.

19. G. Steunebrink, *Kunst, utopie en werkelijkheid*, Tilburg, 1991, pp. 386–412.

20. Adorno, *Negative Dialektik*, Frankfurt am Main, 1973, p. 17 (English translation, by E.B. Ashton, *Negative Dialectics*, New York, 1973, p. 5).

21. Adorno, *Minima Moralia*, Frankfurt am Main, 1970, §29 (translated into English by E.F.N. Jephcott, *Minima Moralia: Reflections from Damaged Life*, London, 1974, §29).

22. Adorno, *Negative Dialektik*, p. 359 (English translation, p. 367.)

23. Ibid., p. 360 (English translation, p. 367). From what follows it will become apparent that I do not share the conception of those who find Auschwitz so incommensurable that it exceeds every form of rationality. Despite the almost unimaginable violence of the event, it is not completely alien to humankind. Its possibility lies in the evil to which no one is completely a stranger. Primo Levi's work is an authentic testimony of this.

24. I am here following Steunebrink, *Kunst*, p. 443.

25. Ibid., p. 440.

26. Recently still, according to the above cited book by Steunebrink.

27. Adorno, *Negative Dialektik*, among other places, pp. 23, 24, 27, 114–15, 150 (English translation, pp. 11–12, 15–16, 108–10, 146–48).

28. Henceforth cited as *Die Religion*. I refer to the edition in the series *Philosophische Bibliothek*, Band 45 (1961). Translated into English by T. Greene and H. Hudson, *Religion Within the Limits of Reason Alone*, Harper & Row, 1960.

29. Hegel, *Vorlesungen über die Philosophie der Geschichte*, edition Suhrkamp, series Studienausgabe, Band 12, pp. 35 and 42 (translated into English by H.B. Nisbet, *Lectures on the Philosophy of World History*, Cambridge, 1975, pp. 69 and 79).

30. Kant, *Idee zu einen allgemeinen Geschichte in weltbürgerlicher Absicht*, in *Kleinere Schriften zur Geschichtsphilosophie, Ethik und Politik* (Edition Philosophische Bibliothek), p. 10. Translated into English by Lewis White Beck, "Idea for a Universal History from a Cosmopolitan Point of View" in *Kant on History*, The Liberal Arts Press, 1957, pp. 11–26, 16.

31. Ibid., 6e Satz, pp. 11–12 (English translation, *Sixth Thesis*, pp. 17–18).

32. J-L. Bruch, *La philosophie religieuse de Kant*, Paris, 1968, p. 45.

33. Ibid., p. 75.

34. Cited by W. Oelmüller, *Die unbefriedigte Aufklärung*, Frankfurt am Main, 1969, p. 227.

35. The central questions of philosophy, What can I know? What must I do? For what can I hope?, according to Kant, flow together in the question, What is the human being? See Kant, Logik, in *Schriften zur Metaphysik und Logik* (edition Weischedel, Band VI), Frankfurt am Main, 1982, p. 448. Translated into English by Robert S. Hartman and Wolfgang Schwarz, *Immanuel Kant: Logic*, New York, The Library of Liberal Arts, 1974, p. 29.

36. See W. Oelmüller, *Aufklärung*, pp. 200ff.

37. The all too well known rule of the universability of maxims is in no way to be understood as a disciplining that produces mere uniformity. The rule is formal in nature. Hence it does not, in a positive manner, prescribe a specific act. It does not say *what* I must *do*, but rather, *how* I must *will*.

38. In *Die Religion*, pp. 25–28 (English translation, pp. 21–23), Kant differentiates between three kinds of human predispositions: the predisposition to *animality* (self-preservation, propagation of the species, and community with other men), the predisposition to *humanity* (self-love through comparison with other men, culture, and so forth) and the predisposition to *personality*.

39. *Die Religion*, p. 28 (English translation, p. 23.)

40. Ibid., p. 29 (English translation, p. 25.)

41. Ibid., p. 30 (English translation, p. 25.)

42. Ibid., pp. 28–29 (English translation, pp. 23–24.) The italics on "is liable to it" are mine.

43. Kants concept of actuality is essentially teleological; see the relevant passages in the *Grundlegung zur Metafysik der Sitten*, AA, 395 (English translation, by Lewis White Beck, *Foundations of the Metaphysics of Morals*, The Library of Liberal Arts, 1959⁸ p. 11), and, of course, the *Critique of Judgment*.

44. *Die Religion*, p. 48 (English translation, p. 40.).

45. Kant's repudiation points out the limitation of his biblical hermeneutics. What Kant rejects is not the core of the Old Testament story of the fall. With respect to Kant's hermeneutic, see L. Heyde: "'. . . door de kennis van goed en kwaad is de mens geworden als een van ons.' Kant en het paradijsverhaal ("through knowledge of good and evil the human being has become one of us," Kant and the story of the Fall)," in K. Boeij et al., *Om de waarheid te zeggen*, Kampen, 1992, pp. 169–82.

46. *Die Religion*, p. 46 (English translation, p. 38), italics mine. Here the primacy of practical reason that so strongly typifies Kant's philosophy is again abundantly evident. It is the apodictic certainty of the ethical ought that leads to a *practical* connection with human *freedom*, instead of to a *theoretical* clarification of evil, thereby circumventing human responsibility.

47. In this sense one can agree with A. Philonenko, who calls radical evil a *limitation originelle* ("an original limitation"), in *L'oeuvre de Kant*, Paris, 1982, Tome II, pp. 224–34.

48. See my opposition to conceptions of evil as completely incommensurable, in note 23.

49. See for example Sartre's definition of existential atheism in *L'existentialisme est un humanisme*, Paris, 1964, p. 21 (English translation, by Philip Mairet, *Existentialism and Humanism*, London, 1973, pp. 27–28), and also his well-known statement *Si Dieu existe, l'homme est néant*, in *Le diable et le bon dieu*, Paris, 1951, p. 267. For a comprehensive discussion of Sartre's atheism, see W. Luijpen, *Fenomenologie en atheisme*, Utrecht/Antwerp, 1963, pp. 319–51. Translated into English as *Phenomenology and Atheism*, Duquesne University Press, Pittsburgh, 1964.

50. On this point I differ from Herman Berger who, in his *Wat is metafysica? Een studie over transcendentie*, Assen/Maastricht 1993, inspired particularly by Whitehead, seems to think in this way (see pp. 143, 159, 168–70). The reference to the Jewish heterodoxy *Zimzum* (see H. Jonas, *Der Gottesbegriff nach Auschwitz*, Frankfurt am Main, 1987) also does not solve the problems in a convincing manner. Kant's opinion, that theodicy in its traditionally rationalistic form does not justify God (but an other being), also holds for this nonetheless beautiful symbol. However, the theme of *Zimzum* can be used to express this very essential thought—namely, that God's existence does not compete with human freedom.

51. See P. Ricoeur, *Finitude et culpabilité, II La Symbolique du mal*, Paris, 1960 (translated into English by Emerson Buchanan, *The Symbolism of Evil*, Boston, 1969). I am here following Th. van Velthoven, *De intersubjectiviteit van het zijn*, Kampen, 1988, particularly pp. 180ff.

52. Th. van Velthoven, *Intersubjectiviteit*, p. 180.

53. Ibidem, pp. 174–75. The text refers to Plotinus, *Enneads I*, VIII, 9.

CHAPTER 5

1. *Tu autem eras interior intimo meo, et superior summo meo*, Augustine, *Confessions*, Book III, chapter VI. This inward dimension is simultane-

ously marked by transcendence, see U. Dhondt, *Hedendaagse denken en christelijk geloof*, Antwerp/Amsterdam, 1981, pp. 17–21.

2. See A. Peperzak, "Op zoek naar ware ervaring," in *Tijdschrift voor Filosofie*, 25 (1964), pp. 607–21.

3. A. Peperzak, "Over waarheid," in *Tijdschrift voor filosofie*, 44 (1982), pp. 33–44.

4. This finitude is fundamental, it encroaches upon Being itself, which is revealed by time which is the "essence" of Sein. See, for instance, S. IJsseling, *Heidegger. Denken en danken. Geven en Zijn*, Antwerp, 1964, particularly pp. 132–40 ("Geschick des Seins").

5. M. Heidegger, *Brief über den Humanismus*, Frankfurt am Main, 1947, p. 36 (English translation, by F.A. Capuzzi and J.G. Gray, *Letter on Humanism*, in *Basic Writings*, edited by David F. Krell, Harper: San Francisco 1978², p. 229).

6. M. Heidegger, *Vom Wesen des Grundes*, Frankfurt am Main, 1955 p. 39 (English translation, by Terrence Malick, *The Essence of Reasons: A bilingual edition incorporating the German text of Vom Wesen des Grundes*, Evanston, Northwestern University Press, 1969, pp. 88–91).

7. *Brief über den Humanismus*, pp. 36–37 (English translation, pp. 229–30).

8. Ibid., p. 37 (English translation, p. 230).

9. Idem.

10. M. Heidegger, *Nietzsche I, Pfullingen*, 1961, p. 366 (English translation, by David F. Krell: *Nietzsche, Volume II: The Eternal Recurrence of the Same*, San Francisco, 1984, p. 106.).

11. M. Heidegger, *Identität und Differenz*, Pfullingen, 1957, p. 71 (English translation, by J. Stambaugh, *Identity and Difference*, Harper & Row, 1969, p. 72).

12. W. Weischedel, *Schriften*, p. 490.

13. *Identität und Differenz*, p. 70 (English translation, p. 72).

14. M. Heidegger, "Wozu Dichter?" in *Holzwege*, Frankfurt am Main, 1950, p. 248 (English translation, by Albert Hofstadter, "What are Poets for?" in *Poetry, Language, Thought*, New York, 1971, pp. 91–142).

15. M. Heidegger, "Die Zeit des Weltbildes" in *Holzwege*, p. 70 (English translation, by William Lovitt, "The Age of the World Picture" in *The Question Concerning Technology and Other Essays*, Harper Torchbooks, 1977, pp. 116–17).

16. Here I almost wholly follow H. Birault's profound and very enlightening interpretation of this passage in "De l'" étre, du divin, des dieux, chez

Heidegger," in H. Birault et al., *L" existence de Dieu*, Doornik, 1963[2], pp. 49–76.

17. Also according to H. Berger. Berger's entire study is interesting, with regard to a critical reflection on Heidegger's concept of metaphysics.

18. M. Heidegger, "Nietzsche's Wort 'Gott ist tot,' " in *Holzwege*, p. 203 (English translation, by William Lovitt, "The Word of Nietzsche," in *The Question Concerning Technology and Other Essays*, Harper Torchbooks, 1977, p. 63).

19. See for instance M. Heidegger *Phänomenologie und Theologie*, Frankfurt am Main, 1970, pp. 13–33 (in part this goes back to a lecture from 1927). For what follows see H. Danner, *Das Gottliche und der Gott bei Heidegger*, Meisenheim am Glan, 1971, particularly pp. 161ff.

20. M. Heidegger, "Nietzsche's Wort 'Gott ist tot,' " in *Holzwege*, p. 203 (English translation, p. 64).

21. H. Birault, *"De l'être,"* pp. 55ff.

22. M. Heidegger, "Nietzsche's Wort 'Gott ist tot,' " in *Holzwege*, p. 230 (English translation, p. 94).

23. M. Heidegger, *Die Technik und die Kehre*, Pfullingen, 1985, p. 46 (English translation, by William Lovitt, "The Turning," in *The Question of Technology and Other Essays*, Harper Torchbooks, 1977, p. 49).

24. The "loss of the gods" does not mean absence *tout court*. The default of God (*Die Fehl Gottes*) has a positive moment, in the way that Being is still present in the withdrawal (*Entzug*). Regarding this see, for instance, H. Birault, *"De l'être,"* pp. 76 ff.

25. This was again made apparent recently, in H. Berger.

26. As IJsseling shows very well, *Geschick* is not to be understood as an "objective" process that plays itself out somewhere above and beyond the thought of the human being (*Heidegger*, p. 138). However, this does not obviate the fact that it remains clearly distinguished from a classic rationalistic position, for example, as Richardson succinctly states: "for Hegel, thought dominates history; for Heidegger history dominates thought" (as cited by IJsseling, *Heidegger*, p. 137).

27. I use the term "seems" to point out what is paradoxical in Heidegger's entire project. With full emphasis on difference, he does not succeed in a fundamental manner in problematizing identity, which determines every claim and every thought (such a problematization would indeed make impossible all thinking). So Heidegger himself, despite the dominance of time, imparts a certain intelligibility to the process of history.

28. M. Heidegger, "Die onto-theologische Verfassung der Metaphysik" in *Identität und Differenz*, Pfullingen, 1957, p. 71 (English translation, p. 73).

29. Hegel, *Phänomenologie des Geistes*, p. 558 (English translation, pp. 486–88).

30. Heidegger in Gespräch, in *Der Spiegel*, 31.05.1976 (translated by Lisa Harries, "The Spiegel Interview" in *Martin Heidegger and National Socialsm: Questions and Answers*, New York 1990, pp. 41–66).

31. Or is the original only to be thought as that which has *always* already passed, definitively? Regarding this, see M. Zarader, *Heidegger et les paroles de l'origine*, Paris, 1986, pp. 207–56.

32. See IJsseling, *Heidegger*, pp. 132–35.

33. I take this expression "positive atheism" from Karl Marx, "Nationalökonomie und Philosophie" (1844), in S. Landshut (ed.), K. Marx, *Die Frühschriften*, Stuttgart, 1971, p. 248 (translated into English by David McLellan, Economic and Philosophical Manuscripts, in *Karl Marx: Early Texts*, Oxford, Basil Blackwell, 1972 pp. 156–57).

34. This expression is taken from W. Oudemans, *De verdeelde mens*, Amsterdam, 1980, particularly pp. 228–259 where with diverse variations it also function with a different meaning.

35. That finitude is merely finite in no way entails a kind of Platonic negation of existence and an overaccentuation of the moment of transcendence. Hopefully this is sufficiently apparent from the whole of our study and particularly from the last paragraph. "Finitude" in no way has a negative connotation. For a contemporary "reprise" of the problem of transcendence, see also O.D. Duintjer, *Rondom metafysica*, Amsterdam 1988.

36. F. Nietzsche, *Die fröhliche Wissenschaft*, KSA, Band 3, p. 481 (English translation, by Walter Kaufmann, *The Gay Science*, New York, 1974, p.181).

37. F. Nietzsche, *Nachgelassene Fragmente*, KSA, Band 13, p. 230.

38. F. Nietzsche, *Also sprach Zarathustra*, KSA, Band 4, p. 172 (English translation, by R. J. Hollingdale, *Thus Spoke Zarathustra*, Penguin, 1969², p. 155).

39. The "possibility" of Nietzsche's project on a moral philosophical level is clearly brought to light in P. Van Tongeren's, *De moraal van Nietzsches moraalkritiek*, Louvain, 1984.

40. The difficulty of philosophically thinking the ideal that Nietzsche formulates has again recently been made abundantly clear to me as a result of R. Van Mil's very fine analysis of certain passages from *Also sprach Zarathustra* in her M.A. thesis at the Catholic University of Nijmegen (*Zarathustra's genezing*, Nijmegen, 1994). It is almost impossible to give a positive genealogy of the assent to existence without reserve which arises in

the work like a flash. *Why* does the repudiation of what is not persist, *what* enables the leap into the absolute affirmation, *how* can a finite being succeed in this, whether this implies that *moral evil* is also affirmed without reservation, all of this remains obscure. It is closer to the *credo quia absurdum* than one would expect. It is all *expressed* in a brilliant way. However, this cannot satisfy those for whom there remains a minimal difference between rhetoric and philosophy.

41. This expression is taken from a lecture by P. Van Tongeren in Nijmegen. My interpretation of Nietzsche is limited to his valuation of finitude. Other elements of his thought are not taken into consideration here.

42. The only *praxis* that remains in Nietzsche is *theory*. Indeed, all action is in one way or the other a negation of what exists which, on account of the ideal, could not be the case. See note 40.

43. This is not only obvious from dominant philosophical trends, but also from more general cultural, ideological, social-political, and ethical characteristics of our time. D. Janicaud gives a penetrating analysis of this in *La puissance du rationnel*, Paris, 1985. See an article of mine that in part returns to this: L. Heyde, "Het huidig bestaan: te "licht" voor een metafysiek?" In G. De Grunt et al. *De weerbarstige werkelijkheid*, Tilburg 1989, pp. 107–22.

44. "Die onto-theologische Verfassung der Metaphysik" in *Identität und Differenz*, Pfullingen, 1957, p. 52 (English translation, p. 55).

45. See Hegel, *Wissenschaft der Logik I*, Suhrkamp Studienausgabe, Band 5, pp. 172–73 (English translation by A.V. Miller, *Hegel's Science of Logic*, Humanities Press, 1990, pp. 154–156; Remark 2: Idealism).

46. Hegel, *Vorlesungen über die Philosophie der Religion*, Band 17, p. 442 (translated into English by the Rev. B. Speirs and J. Burton, *Lectures on the Philosophy of Religion: together with a work on the proofs of the existence of God*, London 1973[3], pp. 259).

47. Hegel, *Wissenschaft der Logik I*, Band 5, p. 172 (English translation, p.154).

48. Hegel, *Vorlesungen über die Philosophie der Religion*, Band 17, p. 465 (English translation, p. 286).

49. Idem.

50. Ibid. p. 443 (English translation, p. 261).

51. Idem (English translation, p. 260).

52. Also the water, the moisture of Thales of Miletus, is not taken in its immediate sense; see Hegel, *Wissenschaft der Logik*, Band 5, p. 172 (English translation, p. 154).

53. As is sufficiently well known, this *rest* is at the same time absolute *movement*.

54. For what follows see L. Heyde, "Filosofie voorbij de grenzen van de politiek" in *Tijdschrift voor Filosofie*, 55 (1983), pp. 80–81 (Philosophy beyond the limits of politics).

55. Hegel, *Vorlesungen über die Beweise vom Dasein Gottes*, Band 17, p. 443 (English translation, as part of the Lectures on the Philosophy of Religion, p. 261).

56. Hegel, *Enzyklopadie der philosophischen Wissenschaften*, par. 50, *Anmerkung* (translated into English by William Wallace, *Hegel's Logic: Part One of the Encyclopaedia of the Philosophical Sciences*, Oxford, 1975, paragraph 50 (p. 81).

57. Idem, "Nichtigkeit" obviously does not mean nullity in an absolute sense. It has a relative meaning and points to the world as being but a moment.

58. This reference is from M. Theunissen in his *Hegels Lehre vom absoluten Geist als theologisch-politisches Traktat*, Berlin, 1970, pp. 221–22.

59. In the first instance, one can think here of the views of Feuerbach.

60. Formulated positively, in symbolic terms: God is greater than our heart. Think of the beautiful passage in Ecclesiastes: "no man can find out the work that God maketh from beginning to end" (3, 11).

61. Think here for example of the open religion and the open morality in H. Bergson's, *Les deux sources de la morale et de la religion*, Paris, 1932 (translated into English by R. Ashley Audra and Cloudesley Brereton, *The Two Sources of Morality and Religion*, London, 1935).

62. That is why he can be symbolically related to the word *void*. See C. Verhoeven, "Rondom de leegte" in *Rondom de leegte*, Utrecht, 1969[6], pp. 155–206.

Cited Literature

Adorno, Th. W. *Minima Moralia*. Frankfurt am Main, 1970. Translated into English by E.F.N. Jephcott, *Minima Moralia: Reflections from a Damaged Life*, London, 1974.

———. *Negative Dialektik*. Frankfurt am Main, 1973. English translation by E.B. Ashton, *Negative Dialectics*, New York, 1973.

Ansel of Canterbury. *Proslogion*. (Vertaling C. Steel, reeks Dixit, Bussum/Antwerp, 1981). Translated into English by J. Hopkins and H. Richardson, volume one in the series *Anselm of Canterbury*, Edwin Mellen Press, 1974.

Aristotle. *De Anima*.

———. *Metaphysics A*.

Augustine, *Confessions*.

Berger, H. *Zo wijd als alle werkelijkheid*. Baarn, 1977.

———. *Wat is metafysica? Een studie over transcendentie*. Assen/Maastricht 1993.

Bergson, H. *Les deux sources de la morale et de la religion*. Paris, 1932. Translated into English by R. Ashley Audra and Cloudesley Brereton, *The Two Sources of Morality and Religion*, London, 1935.

Birault, H., et al. *L'existence de Dieu*. Doornik, Casterman, 1963².

Boer, Th. de *De God van de filosofen en de God van Pascal*. s'-Gravenhage, 1989.

Boey, C. *L'aliénation dans la phénoménologie de l'esprit de G.W.F.Hegel*. Paris-Bruges, 1970.

Bruch, J. L. *La philosophie religieuse de Kant*. Paris, 1968.

Burms, A. and H. De Dijn *De rationaliteit en haar grenzen*. Leuven/Assen/Maastricht, 1986.

Chrétien, J. L. *L'inoubliable et l'inespéré*. Paris, 1991.

Cramer, H. *Gottesbeweise und ihre Kritik*. Frankfurt am Main, 1967.

Danner, H. *Das Göttliche und der Gott bei Heidegger*. Meisenheim am Glan, 1971.

Descartes, R. *Méditations*. ed. Pléiade. English translation by John Cottingham, *Descartes' Meditations*, Cambridge University Press, 1996.

Dhondt, U. *Hedendaagse denken en christelijk geloof*. Antwerp/Amsterdam, 1981.

Diderot, R. *Le Neveu de Rameau*. ed. Gallimard (collection Folio) 1972. Translated and edited by Jacques Barzun and Donald O'Gorman, *Rameau's Nephew*, Geneva, 1973.

Diels. *Fragmenten der Vorsokratiker I*. Berlin, 1956. English translation of and commentary on Heraclitus by T. M. Robinson, *Heraclitus: Fragments*, Toronto, 1987.

Duintjer, O. D. *Rondom metafysica*. Amsterdam, 1988.

Hegel, G.W.F. *Werke in zwanzig Bänden, Theorie Werkausgabe*, Suhrkamp, Frankfurt am Main.

———. *Wie der gemeine Menschenverstand die Philosophie nehme (Band 2)*. Translated into English by H. S. Harris, *How the Ordinary Human Understanding Takes Philosophy* in *Between Kant and Hegel: Texts in the Development of Post-Kantian Idealsm*. SUNY Press, Albany, N.Y.: 1985, 292-310.

———. *Wissenschaft der Logik I (Band 5)*. English translation by A. V. Miller, *Hegel's Science of Logic*, Humanities Press, 1990[2].

———. *Grundlinien der Philosophie des Rechts (Band 7)*. English translation by T. M. Knox, *Hegel's Philosophy of Right*, Oxford University Press, 1969.

———. *Enzyklopädie der philosopischen Wissenschaften (Band 8–10)*. Part one of the *Enzyklopädie* translated into English by T. F. Geraets, W. A. Suchting, and H. S. Harris, *The Encyclopaedia Logic*, Hackett Publishing Company, Indianapolis, 1991; and *Hegel's Logic: Part One of the Encyclopaedia of the Philosophical Sciences*, translated by William Wallace, Oxford, 1975.

———. *Vorlesungen über die Philosophie der Geschicht (Band, 12)*. English translation by H. B. Nisbet, *Lectures on the Philosophy of World History*, Cambridge, 1975.

———. *Vorlesungen über die Beweise vom Dasein Gottes (Band 17)*. Translated into English by the Rev. B. Speirs and J. Burton, *A work on the proofs of the existence of God*, as part of their translation of the *Lectures on the Philosophy of Religion*, London, 1973[3].

———. *Vorlesungen über die Philosophie der Religion (Band 17)*. Translated into English by the Rev. B. Speirs and J. Burton, *Lectures on the Philosophy of Religion*, London, 1973[3].

Hegel, G.W.F. *Phänomenologie des Geistes*, editie Philosophische Bibliothek. English translation by A. V. Miller, *Hegel's Phenomenology of Spirit*, Clarendon Press, Oxford, 1977.

Heidegger, M. *Brief über den Humanismus*. Frankfurt am Main, 1947. English translation by F. A. Capuzzi and J. G. Gray, *Letter on Humanism* in *Basic Writings*, edited by David F. Krell, Harper, San Francisco, 1978[2.]

——. *Nietzsche's Wort "Gott ist tot"* in *Holzwege*. Frankfurt am Main, 1950. English translation by William Lovitt, "The Word of Nietzsche" in *The Question Concerning Technology and Other Essays*, Harper Torchbooks, 1977.

——. *Wozu Dichter?* in: *Holzwege*. Frankfurt am Main, 1950. English translation by Albert Hofstadter, *What are Poets for?* in *Poetry, Language,Thought*, New York, 1971.

——. *Die Zeit des Weltbildes* in *Holzwege*. Frankfurt am Main, 1950. English translation by William Lovitt, *The Age of the World Picture* in *The Question Concerning Technology and Other Essays*, Harper Torchbooks, 1977.

——. *Vom Wesen des Grundes*. Frankfurt am Main, 1955. English translation by Terrence Malick, *The Essence of Reasons: A bilingual edition incorporating the German text of Vom Wesen des Grundes*. Evanston, Northwestern University Press, 1969.

——. *Identität und Differenz*. Pfullingen, 1957. English translation by J. Stambaugh *Identity and Difference*, Harper & Row, 1969.

——. *Nietzsche I and II*. Pfullingen, 1957. Translated into English into four volumes by David Farrell Krell and Frank A. Capuzzi, *Martin Heidegger: Nietzsche-volume I: Will to Power as Art*, 1979; *volume II: The Eternal Recurrence of the Same*, 1984; *volume III: The Will to Power as Knowledge and Metaphysics*, 1987; *Volume IV: Nihilism*, 1982. San Francisco.

——. *Phänomenologie und Theologie*. Frankfurt am Main, 1970.

——. *Die Technik und die Kehre*. Pfullingen, 1985. English translation by William Lovitt, *The Turning* in *The Question of Technology and Other Essays*. Harper Torchbooks, 1977.

——. *Einführung in die Metaphysik*. Tübingen, 1987[5]. English translation by Ralph Manheim, *An Introduction to Metaphysics*, London, 1959.

——. *Die Grundprobleme der Phänomenologie, Gesamtausgabe, Band 24*. English translation by Albert Hofstadter, *Basic Problems of Phenomenology*, Bloomington, Indiana University Press, 1982.

Heidegger in Gespräch, in *Der Spiegel*, 31.05.1976. English translation by Lisa Harries, *The Spiegel Interview* in *Martin Heidegger and National Socialism: Questions and Answers*, New York, 1990.

Heine, H. *Zur Geschichte der Religion und Philosophie in Deutschland* (1834).

Henrich, D. *Der Ontologische Gottesbeweis*. Tübingen, 1967.

Heyde, L. *De verwerkelijking van de vrijheid. Een inleiding in Hegels rechtsfilosofie*. Maastricht/Leuven, 1987.

――. "Staat en maatschappelijk contract" in G. Van Velthoven e.a. *Overheidsbemoeienis*. Deventer, 1982.

――. "Filosofie voorbij de grenzen van de politiek" in *Tijdschrift voor Filosofie*, 55 (1983).

――. "Het huidig bestaan: te 'licht' voor een metafysiek?" in G. De Grunt e.a., *De weerbarstige werkelijkheid*. Tilburg, 1989, pp. 107–22.

――. ". . . door de kennis van goed en kwaad is de mens geworden als een van ons.' Kant en het paradijsverhaal" in K. Boeij e.a(ed.), *Om de waarheid te zeggen*. Kampen, 1992, pp. 169–82.

――. "Subjectiviteit en norm" in *Tijdschrift voor Filosofie*, 56 (1994).

Höffe, O. *Stratagien der Humanität*. Freiburg/Munchen, 1975.

Horkheimer, M., and T. W. Adorno. *Dialektik der Aufklärung*, Frankfurt am Main (Fischer Taschenbuch), 1984. English translation by J. Cumming, *Dialectic of Enlightenment*, Herder, and Herder, 1972.

Husserl, E. *Philosophie als strenge Wissenschaft*. Frankfurt am Main, 1965. Translated into English as "Philosophy as Rigorous Science" in O. Lauer, ed., *Phenomenology and the Crisis of Philosophy*. New York, 1965, pp. 71-147.

――. *Ideen I*. Den Haag, 1976. Translated into English by F. Kersten, *Ideas pertaining to a Pure Phenomenology and to a Phenomenological Philosophy. First Book: General Introduction to a Pure Phenomenology*. The Hague, 1982

Hyppolite, J., *Genèse et structure de la Phénoménologie de l'esprit de Hegel*. Paris, 1978.

IJsseling, S., *Heidegger. Denken en danken, Geven en Zijn*. Antwerp, 1964.

Janicaud, D. *La puissance du rationnel*. Paris, 1985.

Jonas, H. *Der Gottesbegriff nach Auschwitz*. Frankfurt am Main, 1987.

Kant, I. *Logik, in Schriften zur Metaphysik und Logik (edition Weischedel, Band VI)*. Frankfurt am Main, 1982. Translated into English by Robert S. Hartman and Wolfgang Schwarz, *Immanuel Kant, Logic*. New York, The Library of Liberal Art, 1974.

――. *Grundlegung zur Metaphysik der Sitten (edition Philosophische Bibliothek)*. English translation by Lewis White Beck, *Foundations of the Metaphysics of Morals*, The Library of Liberal Arts, 1959[8].

————. *Kritik der praktischen Vernunft* (*edition Philosophische Bibliothek*). Translated into English by Lewis White Beck, *Critique of Practical Reason*, Macmillan, 1993[3].

————. *Kritik der reinen Vernunft* (*edition Philosophische Bibliothek*). Translated into English by Norman Kemp Smith, *Critique of Pure Reason*, Macmillan, London, 1992.

————. *Kritik der Urteilskraft* (*edition Philosophische Bibliothek*). English translation by Werner S. Pluhar, *Critique of Judgement*, Hackett, 1987.

————. *Die Religion* (*edition Philosophische Bibliothek*). Translated into English by T. Greene and H. Hudson, *Religion Within the Limits of Reason Alone*, Harper & Row,1960.

————. "Idee zu einer allgemeinen Geschichte in weltbürgelicher Absicht" in *Kleinere Schriften zur Geschichtsphilosophie, Ethik und Politik* (*edition Philosophische Bibliothek*). Translated into English by Lewis White Beck, "Idea for a Universal History from a Cosmopolitan Point of View" in *Kant: On History*. The Liberal Arts Press, 1957, pp. 11–26.

————. "Über den Gemeinspruch: Das mag in der Theorie richtig sein, taugt aber nicht für die Praxis" in *Kleinere Schriften zur Geschichtsphilosophie, Ethik und Politik* (*edition Philosophische Bibliothek*). Translated into English by E. B. Ashton, *On the Old Saw: That May be right in Theory but it Won't Work in Practice*. Philadelphia, 1974.

Karskens, M. "The development of the opposition subjective versus objective in the 18th century" in *Archiv für Begriffsgeschichte*, 35(1992) 214-56.

Kerken, L. van der *Inleiding tot de fundamentele filosofie*. Kapellen, 1969.

Labarrière, P.J. *Introduction à une lecture de la Phénoménologie de l'esprit de Hegel*. Paris, 1979.

Leibniz, G. W. *Principes de la nature et de la grâce*. Opera, ed. Gerhardt, t. VI. Translated into English by Roger Ariew and Daniel Garber, "Principles of Nature and Grace, Based on Reason" in *G. W. Leibniz: Philosophical Essays*. Hackett, 1989, pp. 206–13.

Léonard, A. *La foi chez Hegel*. Paris, 1970.

Levi, P. *Is dit een mens?* Amsterdam, 1988[5].

Levinas, E. *Totalité et Infini*. La Haye, 1961. English translation by Alphonso Lingis, *Totality and Infinity*, Duquesne University Press, 1969.

Lübbe, H. (Hrsg.) *Wozu Philosophie?* Berlin-New York, 1978.

Luijpen, W. *Phenomenologie en atheisme*. Utrecht/Antwerp, 1963. Translated into English as *Phenomenology and Atheism*, Duquesne University Press, Pittsburgh, 1964.

Mansfeld, J. *Heraclitus, Fragments*, bezorgd, vertaald en toegelicht. Amsterdam, 1979.

Marx, K. "Nationalökonomie und Philosophie" (1844) in S. Landshut (ed.), K. Marx, *Die Frühschriften*. Stuttgart, 1971. Translated into English by David McLellan, "Economic and Philosophical Manuscripts" in *Karl Marx: Early Texts*. Basil Blackwell, Oxford, 1972.

————. "Luther als Schiedsrichter zwischen Strauss und Feuerbach" in K. Marx and F. Engels, *Werke I*. Dietz Verlag, Berlin, 1974. Translated into English by D. McLellan, "Luther as Judge between Strauss and Feuerbach" in *Karl Marx: early texts*, Basil Blackwell, Oxford, 1972

Moors, M. *De Godsidee bij Kant. Haar bepalings-structuur in de voorkritische en kritische transcendentaalfilosofie*. Leuven, 1986, XLII + 602 pp.

Nietzsche, F. *Also sprach Zarathustra, KSA Band 4*. English translation by R. J. Hollingdale, *Thus Spoke Zarathustra*, Penguin, 1969[2].

————. *Die Fröhliche Wissenschaft, KSA Band 3*. English translation by Walter Kaufman, *The Gay Science*, New York, 1974.

————. *Nachgelassene Fragmente 1887–1889, KSA Band 13*.

Oelmüller, W. *Die unbefriedigte Aufklärung*. Frankfurt am Main, 1969.

Oudemans, W. *De verdeelde mens*. Amsterdam, 1980.

Peperzak, A. *Verlangen. De Huidige mens en de vraag naar heil*. Bilthoven, 1971.

————. *Erotiek*. Nijmegen, 1992.

————. "Op zoek naar ware ervaring," in *Tijdschrift voor Filosofie* 25 (1964). pp. 607–21.

————. "Over waarheid" in *Tijdschrift voor Filosofie* 44 (1982), pp. 33–44.

Perreijn, W. *Kants ethiek tussen ervaring en apriori*. Tilburg, 1993.

Peursen, C. A. van *De Naam die geschiedenis maakt: het geheim van de bijbelse godsnamen*. Kampen, 1991.

Philonenko, A. *L'oeuvre de Kant*. Paris, 1982.

Plato. *Gorgias*.

Plotinus. *Enneaden*.

Raeymaeker, L. De *De metafysiek van het zijn*. Antwerp-Nijmegen, 1947.

Reijen, W. van *Filosofie als kritiek*. Alphen a/d Rijn/Brussels, 1981.

Ricoeur, P. *Finitude et culpabilité II La Symbolique du mal*. Paris, 1960. Translated into English by Emerson Buchanan, *The Symbolism of Evil*, Boston, 1969.

Ritter J. (hrsg.), *Historisches Wörterbuch der Philosophie*.

Sartre, J.-P. *Le diable et le bon Dieu*. Paris, 1951.

————. *L'existentialisme est un humanisme*. Paris, 1964. English translation by Philip Mairet, *Existentialism and Humanism*, London, 1973.

Scheltens, D. F. *De tijd van God*. Antwerp, 1972.

Schulz, W. *Der Gott der neuzeitlichen Metaphysik*. Pfullingen, 1957.

Spaemann, R. *Die Frage nach der Bedeutung des Wortes "Gott"* in *Internationale Katholische Zeitschrift I* (1972) 62.

Steenbergen, F. Van *Le problème de l'existence de Dieu dans les écrits de St. Thomas d'Aquin*. Louvain-la-Neuve, 1980.

Stegmaier, W. *Substanz. Grundbegriff der Metaphysik*. Stuttgart-Bad Cannstatt, 1977.

Steunebrink, G, *Kunst, utopie en werkelijkheid*. Tilburg, 1991.

Theunissen, M. *Hegels Lehre vom absoluten Geist als theologisch-politisches Traktat*. Berlin, 1970.

Thomas Aquinas. *Summa contra Gentiles*. Translated into English by Vernon J. Bourke, Notre Dame/London, 1957.

————. *Summa Theologiae*, I.

Tongeren, P. Van *De moraal van Nietzsches moraalkritiek*. Leuven, 1984.

Velthoven, Th. Van *De intersubjectiviteit van het zijn*. Kampen, 1988.

Vergote, A. *Interprétation du language religieux*. Paris, 1974.

Verhoeven, C. *Rondom de leegte*. Utrecht, 1969[6].

Visscher, J. De *De immorele mens*. Bilthoven, 1975.

Voltaire. *Candide*.

Weischedel, W. *Der Gott der Philosophen*, Darmstadt, 1983[2].

Weissmahr, B. *Philosophische Gotteslehre*. Stuttgart, 1983.

Welte, B. *Religionsphilosophie*. Freiburg-Basel-Wenen, 1978.

Zaradar, M. *Heidegger et les paroles de l'origine*. Paris, 1986.

About the Author

Ludwig Heyde (1941) is professor of metaphysics and epistemology at the Catholic University Nijmegen. He has published various contributions in the areas of the history of modern philosophy, ethics, and metaphysics, among others *De verwerkelijking van de vrijheid. Een inleiding in Hegels rechtsfilosofie* (1987) [*The Actualization of Freedom. An Introduction to Hegel's Philosophy of Right*].

Index

Abraham, xiii, 30
Adam, 113
Adorno, Th. W., 101, 102, 103, 104, 155, 156
Anselm of Canterbury, Saint, xii, xiv, 36, 44–48, 53, 62 f., 73, 80, 148, 149, 150
Aristotle, 2, 49, 57, 74, 151
Augustine, Saint, 117, 158

Barth, Karl, 121, 147
Bauer, B., 140 f.
Berger, H., 151, 158, 160
Bergson, H., 163
Birault, H., 126, 127, 159, 160
Boeij, K., 157
Boethius, 100
Boey, C., 146
Bruch, J.-L., 157
Burms, A., 155

Calley, Lt., 83
Candide, 96
Chrétrien, J. L., 57, 151
Comte, A., xi
Cramer, H., 148, 149
Cyclops, The, 101 f.

Danner, H., 160
De Boer, Th., 145, 147
De Dijn, H., 155
Diels, 151
De Grunt, G., 162

de Jong, A., xvii
De Raeymaeker, 155
Derrida, J., 147
De Visscher, J., 83, 154
Descartes, R., xii, 9, 36, 45, 48–57, 62 f., 66, 73, 80, 123, 127, 141, 145, 148, 150, 151, 152
Desmond, W., xi–xv, xvii, xviii
Diderot, F., 12, 14, 15, 21, 27, 146, 147
Dhondt, U., 159
Duintjer, O. D., 161

Engels, F., 152

Feuerbach, L., 20, 22 f., 152, 163
Fichte, J. G., 153

Gaunilo, 150
Goethe, J. W., 105

Harmsen, A., xvii
Hegel, G.W.F., xii, xiii, xiv, xv, 3, 5, 6, 10–16, 18 f., 21f., 24–26, 30, 36, 43, 45, 48, 57, 62 f., 73, 88–91, 101–103, 104, 115, 119, 123 f., 127, 130 f., 136–140, 142, 145, 146, 147, 148, 149, 151, 153, 154, 155, 156, 161, 162, 163
Heidegger, M., xi, xiii, xiv, 7, 32, 39, 49, 55, 119–132, 136, 147, 148, 149, 150, 155, 159, 160, 161
Heine, H., 80, 153

Henrich, D., 48, 150, 151
Heraclitus, 57, 151
Herder, J. G., 105
Heyde, L., 146, 147, 157, 162, 163
Hinske, N., 148,
Hobbes, T., 52
Höffe, O., 147,
Hölderin, J.-C., 129,
Hollak, J., 147
Horkheimer, M., 101, 156
Husserl, E., 34, 147, 148
Hyppolite, J., 146

IJsseling, S., 159, 160, 161
Isaac, xiii, 30

Jacob, xiii, 30
Jacobi, F. H., 127
Janicaud, D., 162
Jesus Christ, 30
JHWH, 29
Jonas, H., 158

Kant, I., xi, xiii, 4, 20, 27, 36, 41,
   45, 49, 56, 61–92, 96, 104–111,
   114, 118, 121, 123, 127, 139,
   145, 149, 152, 153, 154, 156,
   157, 158
Karksens, M., 150
Kierkegaard, S., 126, 127

Labarrière, P. J., 146
Lampe, 81
Lanzmann, C., 94
Leibniz, G.W.F., 39, 42, 105, 148,
   149
Levi, P., 95, 155, 156
Léonard, A., 146
Levinas, E., 81, 93, 147, 153, 155
Lingis, A., 155
Luijpen, W., 158
Luther, M., 152

Marx, K., xi, 152, 161
Mersenne, M., 52, 53
Moors, M., 153

Nietzsche, F., xi, xiv, 1, 7, 119–121,
   133–135, 147, 161, 162

Odysseus, 101 f.
Oelmüller, W., 157
Oudemans, W., 161

Pangloss, Dr., 96
Pascal, B., 29, 33, 122, 126, 127,
   145, 147
Paul, Saint, 124
Peperzak, A., 151, 159
Perreijn, W., 154
Philonenko, A., 158
Plato, 3, 49, 57 f., 75, 155, 161
Plotinus, 114, 158

Richardson, W., 160
Ricoeur, P., 158
Rijnders, R., xvii
Ritter, J., 148
Rorty, R., 147

Sartre, J.-P., 1, 58, 111, 158
Schelling, F.W.J., 153
Scheltens, D. F., 155
Schulz, W., 55 f., 150, 151, 154
Spaemann, R., 155
Spinoza, B., 35
Steel, C., 47, 150
Stegmaier, W., 150
Steunebrink, G., 156

Thales of Miletus, 162
Thomas Aquinas, Saint, xii, xiv,
   37–39, 41, 43, 47, 49, 57, 62, 80,
   100, 104, 116, 149, 151, 155
Theunissen, M., 163

van Dyck, J., xvii
Voltaire, 96, 155
Van der Kerken, L., 148
Van Mil, R., 161
van Peursen, C. A., 148
Van Reijen, W., 156
van Steenbergen, F., 149
Van Tongeren, P., 161, 162
van Velthoven, Th., 158

Vergote, A., 148
Verhoeven, C., 163

Weischedel, W., 154, 159
Weissmahr, B. 149
Welte, B., 149
Whitehead, A. N., 158

Zarader, M., 161